Just Throw the Dart

Just Throw the Dart

Richard Amiss

Foreword by Nancy Franklin

RESOURCE *Publications* · Eugene, Oregon

JUST THROW THE DART

Resource Publications
An Imprint of Wipf and Stock Publishers
199 W. 8th Ave., Suite 3
Eugene, OR 97401

www.wipfandstock.com

PAPERBACK ISBN: 978-1-5326-4561-7
HARDCOVER ISBN: 978-1-5326-4562-4
EBOOK ISBN: 978-1-5326-4563-1

Manufactured in the U.S.A.   06/15/18

This book is dedicated to my wife Beth who is the love of my life and who suggested that I write a book, so I did. She has lightened up my life is countless ways.

Contents

Foreword

Metaphors are all around us. Some of us can see them and experience them; others of us don't seem to have that gift. Holy books are filled with metaphors, and those same books lead us to living better, deeper and more fulfilling lives. Much of art is pure metaphor. Play therapy is a never ending source of metaphor, and, as Richard Amiss has trained more and more in play therapy, he has embraced metaphors more and more.

When I first met Amiss over five years ago, he was an accomplished therapist who could diagnose and determine a therapy treatment plan in a manner of minutes. He can still do that, but he now can see the metaphors that are obviously in front of him. How rich our lives become as we see those metaphors all around us! Practicing play therapy will do that for a person because children's language is not words; it is play and metaphors.

Someone once said, "Sometime a cigar is just a cigar," and that is true. And, yet, sometimes a cigar is a symbol for something else and is used in ways that have little to do with tobacco. Some can see that; some cannot.

Metaphors are for sharing with others and, as we share them, those who are with us can float into that world of imagination and creativity and help add to or enrich the metaphor according to their outlook on life. Who knew a lost dart could be something more than a game of hide and seek? Who knew a lily pad floating down a stream could be more than a lily pad? Who knew?

And that is what this book and metaphors are all about; wondering, "Who knew!"

—Nancy Franklin

I'm so grateful for being able to have the experience of being a therapist and for all the people who allowed me into part of their lives. I want to thank all of my children for making my life better and for being great teachers. Dr. Frank Emmett gave me a chance to work at the Ecumenical Center for Education, Counseling and Health and gave me a great opportunity. Thanks to my parents may they rest in peace who were teaching me to love myself and to know that I can! My mother told me there is nothing that you and Jesus can't go through together. To all my siblings and for our memories I am grateful for their love.

Introduction

This book is really about my work with people in therapy over the course of twenty one years. We all think forward or backward in a linear fashion. However what works best for me is to use metaphors to explain my point to other people or to teach. In truth I do not feel that I am as much of a psychotherapist now as I am a teacher. I have worked with all types of people in all age ranges from 3 and up in individual, couples, family, parent consultations, play and group therapy. While I don't assign myself to a specific modality exclusively, I would say that my approach is more spiritual at the core than anything else.

I have used material from a variety of books on counseling and psychology, but I feel like I took a long jump toward spirituality when I started reading books on Christian and Jewish mysticism, the chakras, the Tao, The Bhagavad Gita, Shamans, works by Don Miguel Ruiz and Anita Moorjani just to name a few masterful teachers. Once I started reading books on spirituality I never looked back because I believe all human problems are of the spirit more than anything else. Then from there I just continued and it's been pedal to the metal ever since. I apply everything I read to myself and then bring it into therapy.

This book is about metaphors and how they apply to different situations in people's lives. Metaphors make things easier to understand. The brunt of therapy is heavy so in order to make things clear metaphors are like a flash card or billboard to give to the client to take with them. Why leave metaphors within the confines of the therapy encounter? Why not use them in an everyday practice as an affirmation or as a theme that helps us approach a challenge. Each of the metaphors are intended simply to help in a simple way.

Chapter One

Just Throw the Dart

When words are pictures it seems to be easier for me to communicate. I might say to myself that many times I get an aha from someone I am working with or I get an aha in my head and use it later on. There are so many messages being declared in the context of therapy besides just words. Body language is often thought to be how most of what is being said is shared. So much of my experience is of a heaviness after being in sessions all day long so I believe my brain came up with an idea to adapt and that idea was metaphors. I don't know which one came first so as I remembered them I just stored them away. At the time of this book I have been doing therapy for 21 years. When I had been doing it for 5 years it seemed like 20 or more years at it was a long time and now I am here. However, metaphors didn't really come to me more so until the last few years. Now it seems metaphors and storytelling are the only way I do therapy unless its play therapy which has its own formulary if you will. Still even in that context life provides metaphors when the therapy is more about play than it is about words.

People have brought many gifts to therapy without knowing it because I learned a long time ago that everyone you come into contact with is a teacher. So we are giving each other messages without even knowing it to an extent. One time I was working with a young boy in play therapy who was in elementary school. When I approach play therapy I do so within the confines of personality types and constructs. Constructs are words like connect, count, courage and capable. Personality types are comfort, pleaser, control and superior. Then I go from there and try to detect how this particular child is being challenged because life is challenging us all the time. Sometimes there is a part of us that is being challenged or parts. I will share more about that in a later chapter. I had seen this child who I will call Luis. Luis was able to connect really well meaning he felt comfortable being in therapy from the get go and was engaged in the playing. In play therapy there are many options of categories for kids to play in. On this one particular day Luis and I were in a play room across the hall from the playroom I had been playing in. The playroom I had been using with him was in use so I had to go across the hall. As much as possible we tried in our practice to provide as much continuity as possible. However one day I had to switch rooms because the room I usually use was occupied by another therapist. No big deal. Even though each room is equipped with the same toys, one room has more windows and the other room has more floor space. The room we had been using has 4 darts of red and yellow each, but the room we were in only had 3 of each.

In order to proceed Luis had to find the other two darts because he assumed there were four of each color in this room too. There was not. However, my job is to reflect and track what the child is doing without directing. So he immediately became frustrated because he could not find the other two darts and he could not play because he could not find those darts. It wasn't my job to tell him we didn't have that many in that room. Frantically he said he could not play darts until he found the other two missing darts. He began looking everywhere and searching through all the toys so he could find the darts and play. Noticing his frustration, anxiety and that worry filled his head, I said "you seem really upset, I wonder what would happen if you just threw the dart." He ignored me and kept circling the room as if he would find the other two darts. I made the statement again noticing this time that he had the darts in his hand "I wonder what would happen if you just threw the dart" and so again he ignored me and his anxiety ramped up. At this point he was completely in his head with worry and anxiety as he was a leaf and his worry was the wind. This was a kid who loved to have fun and he enjoyed playing with others, but not having those two darts was totally derailing him. So then a third time I said "I wonder what would happen if you just threw the dart" with more emphasis in my voice. He stopped what he was doing, looked at the dartboard and threw a dart with gusto and you could hear the dart hit the board. Suddenly he smiled looking at the dart on the dartboard and then looked at me. Then he began to throw the rest of the darts one by one. To me a miraculous thing occurred before my eyes. Luis got out of his head and into his heart as he became spontaneous and stopped worrying about the other darts he was looking for in the first place. Those other two darts were never there. The rest of the session he just concentrated on playing darts and having fun.

His fears were keeping him in his head and he was locked in on worrying about finding those other darts that were never there. When he was afraid he was in the future because he didn't think he was going to be able to play. When he got out of his head he played. So this metaphor poses the question: are we following what is in our head or following what is in our hearts? Being in our head keeps us in the past and keeps us in the future, but we only really live in the present moment. By his experiences he was taught to be afraid of everything going wrong in the future. In his right brain he pictured not being able to play darts and everything going terrible. When he did what he wanted, which was to play darts instead of worrying, he was much more comfortable in the session and was able to leave with peace of mind.

So the example was set. So much of our moving forward in life is set between the parenthesis of the past and future. So we can choose to be frozen or move forward not based on experiences we have been through, but more so through trusting our own intuition. Fear keeps us frozen in the middle of our own past and our own future. We can ask ourselves what keeps us frozen in the present? The fears we have keep us in the past and future. Neither of these places are locations we actually live in. Can we be as spontaneous as a baby or a puppy in front of a mirror? We are trained to live in the past and the future. With the way life is structured we have to plan, we have to be connected to the internet, everything is on the go and as fast as we can, we chase after happiness and in this frame of mind we will always be pursuing.

In all his looking for the dart Luis was pursuing happiness when it was already in his hand. All he had to do was throw the dart. I think about all the energy that was spent worrying about where the other darts were and the anguish that was on his face. When he threw the dart he smiled. He was happy. However, I was struck by this lesson and could see how much someone being stuck in their head could keep them from moving forward. Later after several sessions and consulting with his parent, we agreed that the child's biggest fear was of everything going wrong in the future. So the more structure and consistency he is afforded the more we hope he will settle down. Life does not always provide this for us though I have seen the point is important enough. When we can, learning how to make choices from our own intuition and from our heart seem to be the best measures of someone making choices in their own best interest.

Sometimes we just will serve ourselves better if we just throw the dart. We are not able to control our future, but only can plan in the present for the best possible outcome. I often encourage people to follow their intuition, gut or third eye chakra, which is in my opinion the Holy Spirit. Kids usually are not in their heads at birth and only start to spend more time their heads based upon circumstances often beyond their control such as when they are trying to get rewards and avoid consequences. Life is wrought with triggers that send us into our head and so we are trained to be there. The mind is a great tool, but a lousy master I once read. So much of life it seems is going from being in our hearts when we are just coming into this world and shortly thereafter moving into living in our heads because this is the demand the world places upon us. Life becomes serious leaving fun and laughter in the back seat.

And so it can become this way with our lives spiritually. Worry and anxiety like in this child's head takes the fun and laughter away. The way back into our hearts is to live in the present and keep the seriousness in our lives in balance.

What darts are you holding in your hand? What things are you worried about that keep you frozen and in your head? Is it speaking your truth or following the inspirations of your heart? Is it not conforming to how everyone else wants your life to go? Is it being in charge of other people's happiness or being afraid to be happy yourself? The darts in your own hand are the things you are worried about in your life. It's it is life's way of letting you know of what is going on inside you so you cannot be blinded by judgment of others or self. When we hold darts in our hand it keeps us blind because fear obscures our view of ourselves and others. Do what makes you happy. Throw the dart and see what happens. What is your bullseye? Aim for that.

Chapter Two

Fireflies

When I was a teenager I remember walking into my dad's office on a weekend afternoon and saying "I'm bored." His answer was "go outside and commute with nature." Not the answer I really wanted. I didn't know what I wanted to hear. I was just bored. I wanted to be entertained and I realize that this was really not an issue when I was a younger kid. When I was a younger kid I remember waking up early on a Saturday morning and running out of the door of the home where my family lived in Georgia with our Black Lab named Trip. I ran around outside and played in the woods by myself and ran through bridle paths on our land we were fortunate enough to have. I would play imaginary football games in the backyard we had, which was the equivalent of a small football field. Of course every time I played a game I won. I pretended to be the quarterback or defensive back intercepting a pass. I always had fun and life flowed and I brought my imagination to life. I wasn't bored.

When I had become older it seemed like I wanted life to entertain me a little more and perhaps didn't have the gumption to use my imagination as much as I did before. So I reported to my father that I was bored. "Commute with nature" I replied? Then he would tell me "nature was proof of God." "Just go outside and look. The proof is all around you" he said. In my mind I thought the fact that nature is outside was just that nature was outside. It meant nothing else. And for many years I knew where he was coming from intellectually although I did not feel it inside. In my late forties I had more time for myself because my kids were much older and I was left to myself. What do I do now? I rediscovered my love for nature so I started running again and riding my bike. I loved being outside and I met my wife who also loved being outside in nature. She too had spent much of her childhood out in nature riding horses and such and loved being outside. Part of the reason God put us together was because of our love of nature.

So high on the list of things to do or enjoy is being in nature. What is in nature? Everything! Fireflies are out in nature. Let me narrow my focus down to them. Nature is just another way of looking at the possibility of life and the ways it can manifest whether it is a hurricane, a forest or a firefly. Looking at fireflies can be momentarily mystifying like looking at a Christmas tree. Something about seeing fireflies is mesmerizing. How does a bug light up? I thought only light bulbs give off light. Firefly's just fly and light up.

All of our lives we are like fireflies. It seems like when I walk in the park with my wife in the springtime they start to show up out of nowhere. What I see is that they always seem to be rising from the ground. They always seem to be ascending. Such I believe is the way our lives are. When we love ourselves we are not judging others or ourselves. We are free to love ourselves. Our light then shines and we ascend. So I thought that fireflies come it seems from the ground and they have moments when they light up and moments when they don't. We keep ascending from birth to death and then we are no more in this life.

We are born and then we have moments when we shine and don't shine. We are ever ascending to death and then we are no more and we have faded away. Fireflies are here to shine and when we shine we are not living in our minds. We are living in our hearts. We all have moments of darkness when we are not shining. It could be a move to a new location, the loss of a family member, the failing of a class or an injury. Life is challenging. The point I would like to make is that to judge ourselves or others or to think we are not loveable is like our light is not shining. We have been taught to judge ourselves because that is in our training as kids and our parents don't even know they are handing down what they know and then years down the road we try to figure out why we are the way we are. If we can live our lives our light will shine when we love ourselves and when we don't judge others or ourselves. How does this happen? The traps that are set for ourselves are those of pride and self-pity. When we engage in these activities or processes our light will not shine. What causes pride and self-pity? Fear. In order to handle fear we try to convince ourselves that we are not as good as others or we try to convince ourselves that we are better than others. When we do this we do not shine. We are taught not to shine. It is our birthright to shine though we may not think we have that right. Evermore we are ascending to our death. I believe we are taught how to do this much more than we are taught to love ourselves. What does loving ourselves really look like? It's a firefly that is shining. How many moments in our lives will our light shine? In reality we blink off and on. We are the ones who decide to shine our light. However, we are trained to think that this decision is in another's hands. So we can blink a little or we can blink a lot. It is up to us.

Maybe someone won't like it if we blink, if we light up. Maybe we don't think we deserve to light up. Maybe we will get hurt if we light up. Maybe someone won't love us if we don't light up. I don't think fireflies have these thoughts. Thank God otherwise we may never or hardly ever see them. They are doing what they came here to do. What did you come here to do? A firefly's time is always running out. Do you think they are worried about this? When we love ourselves we are deciding to be a firefly and let our light shine. The only light we have is love. Each firefly is truly flying by itself. Each is alone. Each decides to let their light shine. All are separate and part of creation and I don't think I have ever heard anyone complain when they see a firefly. They are magical. We are magical always, but what blocks us is fear. Love is the magic of life. When we are walking we see a firefly and then another and then there are a bunch of them. The walk becomes more enchanting.

I don't think fireflies have low self-worth and worry. They don't ask for permission. Are fireflies too cautious? No one ever says "look at the firefly. Its looks so timid." No firefly gets out alive and neither do anyone of us. Each firefly is to be itself. It is the same for us so the biggest question is what is keeping us from loving ourselves? That answer is what is keeping us from loving ourselves. In truth the firefly has moments when you see it then you don't.

So there are times when others see us at our best or they don't. Some people pretend to shine, but this light is duller than others. Have you ever seen someone who lights up a room? Yes you have and I have too. Fireflies remind me in the subtlest way that there is a God. Watching someone you love breath while asleep to me is proof there is God and there is life. When we are feeling low we can remember we are like a firefly that isn't lit up and when we are feeling happy we can know that there is love that is being expressed. Notice all the fireflies in life around you. Really they are everywhere if you can see with your heart.

Chapter Three

The Storm

Lately I have observed the weather more so because of a recent trip to the Caribbean. Before leaving I start checking the weather ahead of time by a couple of weeks. One hurricane was out there so that grabbed my attention. Obviously we want to avoid a storm such as this. However nature can be thrilling or there wouldn't be storm chasers. Sometimes nature is way more powerful than we give it credit for. During Hurricane Kate in 1985 I ventured out to see what a hurricane was really like because one had recently come close to where I was living in the Florida panhandle although it was not a direct hit. Kate was a direct hit and it was dare I say just a category 2.

Well I observed mother nature's force up close when I drove out to the airport and all the planes were upside down and there were live power lines everywhere. The barometric pressure was so low that it cracked my windshield. With all this happening at night it made it a challenge just to get home safe. When I finally made it home after driving around fallen trees that made the road an obstacle course, I saw that a giant oak tree that was right next to my dog run was out of the ground. It had smashed said dog run and kennel. I had placed my dog in the house before I left.

So when I see all these category 4 and 5 storms hit the Caribbean I take notice. Once when in St. Lucia a hurricane was three hundred miles away my wife and I observed ten foot swells while the sun was still out. We could hear the waves crashing down at night. They boomed like thunder!

Each of us will be challenged in our lives many times. I read recently that God challenges us. Those challenges can come in many forms such as losing connections with people we lost or by not feeling alive somehow anymore. I think little kids are so alive that they don't even know it whereas if you live long enough so many things happen that can make you feel less alive. Challenges can come in many forms like in the need to create or express feelings and in learning to make the best decisions that benefit us the most based upon love. So often we are programmed to make decisions based upon fear and this usually doesn't bode well for us. If I have fear in my body because I see a bear this is good because the fear is my body trying to survive. If I have fear in my mind that is destructive and inhibits our decision making.

Maybe the storm could be that we believe that something is wrong with us or that we are not loveable. Imagine someone who was abandoned at birth and who knew this fact and that they were adopted. They could be the most loving person in the whole world and still grapple with this thought, "Why did you leave me. Wasn't I good enough to keep"? Then in order to be good enough to keep your focus was on keeping that from happening again. How do you do that? What I have seen is that people will give their power away by trying to make other people happy. By putting themselves in charge of another person's happiness they believe the illusion that they are in charge of another person's happiness. When we give our power away we will not be able to make good decisions that benefit us the most because we are making decisions based upon fear and this will lead to a less than optimal outcome for one's self and others.

We then will not speak our truth, but instead will speak out of fear. We won't be open and honest in our communication and we will not communicate our feelings with ease. We won't speak authentically and our will to overcome our challenges will be squashed. We will not be at peace. While all of this is happening within ourselves we are not able to listen to our inner wisdom because we will be externally focused. I believe everyone has an internal navigational system. Often people in therapy are looking to me for answers and more than anything else I direct them back to their own intuition so that they can trust their inner guidance to make the right choice. People ask what is the difference between judgment or intuition? Fear never has a peaceful answer. Our intuition provides us with a peaceful answer. This is the third eye chakra or as I like to call it, The Holy Spirit.

With all this in mind it is very challenging to be connected to God. You could call all of this the storm. The storm is the result of one, two or several of our chakras being challenged. Someone once said that to not use the word struggle, which creates a feeling of depletion. Instead use the word challenge because some part of us is being challenged. It is easy to think that we cannot withstand the storm when it is happening to us. We can however decide to be the storm instead. How do we become the storm? We can look at all the chakras which in the most simplistic way are statements about our powers. They are I Am, I feel, I do, I love, I speak, I see and I know.

We can start by becoming connected to ourselves by connecting through nature, yoga, prayer or whatever grounds us. We have a right to be here just like a star or a tree. We can stand for what is important to us and stand on the ground with our own two feet. We can nurture our bodies and be thankful for the challenges that help us to grow. We can work on healthy boundaries, be passionate, value ourselves more, appreciate strengths, look for opportunities to grow and be at peace with ourselves. Expressing our feelings and our creativity are also essential to who we are as a person. When we can be who we truly are through creating music, art or whatever we feel our talents are, we are creating from what we feel. This in turn leads us to become better at decision making, having an ego that has a strong identify and to make decisions that benefit us out of love for our self.

We can choose to love ourselves and accept ourselves for who we are. I have for years now asked four questions at the end of every intake session.

1. Do you like yourself?
2. Do you love yourself?
3. Do you accept yourself?
4. Do you forgive yourself?

The answers to these questions tell me more about a person's relationship with themselves than any other questions I ask. Rarely do people say that they love themselves. My mother told me for much of my life to be good to myself. The lesson was really love yourself and love your neighbor as yourself. However people are generally baffled as to what this means. Weathering the storms in our life becomes more challenging when we don't love ourselves. Nearly all people I've seen don't know how to describe themselves loving themselves. It is like they are mystified by this. I believe that we are generally made to live according to what is going on outside of ourselves. It starts with our parents, teachers, peers, media and on and on. By the time we get trained by all of these people how to be and to act we forget who we are. We become so full of judgments of ourselves and so many other people and we lose touch with our spirit. We get to the point where speaking our own truth is foreign to us. We become so full of judgments when we tell people or ourselves what we should, ought, need, have to, must, got to, supposed to, you better and with all these judgments we end up feeling angry, anxious, afraid, shame and guilt. How can we ever speak our truth and feel like we have the right to speak our truth if our mind is cluttered with all this judgment? Speaking our truth is one way to overcome the storm and not speaking our truth is one way the storm overcomes us.

Each of us I believe is being guided by what is inside of us. I believe The Holy Spirit is the same as the third eye chakra talked about in Hindu religion. We are constantly being guided internally. Some people say we are guided by our heart and make our decisions from there. Whatever works! I believe people often have most of the answers they are asking questions about. It is wise to get answers from wise people or from books. However we go through the day and are constantly making decisions. Many times people ask me questions about when to come in for the next session or how often do I think they should be here in session with me. I turn it back on them and ask them. I encourage people to look for the answers inside of themselves already and practice at it. Practice following your intuition and notice it as being there. What is the difference between making decisions based upon judgment or intuition I am often asked? The difference between the two is that decisions made upon intuition produce peace while making decisions based upon judgment produces fear. If we don't use our intuition the storm grows bigger and if we use our intuition we are the storm.

We all have the right to be connected to God. I believe we are going through a huge global transformation and are beginning to realize how connected we all are. I believe religion will have less of an influence in the future and spirituality will have a greater influence. You can have a church full of people, but they can all have and usually do have different views about who God is and what God does. When I read Jesus Calling, an outstanding devotional by Sarah Young there is a scripture about Jesus being in unapproachable light. I like that. Here is God asking me to approach Him with confidence even though He is so bright I can't even look at Him directly like Moses couldn't look at God directly. I like how Anita Moorjani says we are all always connected rather than saying we have to do specific things to be connected to God. I also like how Jesus tells us that He is watching us all the time and is available all the time. I think it's common though to feel disconnected when things are not going our way. Let's tell like it is. Life's sucks sometimes. The challenge here is to stay connected to God. Can we be open to divine wisdom and can we speak words that empower our spirit. Can we go five minutes without judging ourselves or others?

There are many ways to feed ourselves spiritually. Our spirit needs a steady diet because life can make a steady diet of us. Whether it's frustrations with career, relationships, our own feelings or where we are in life just to name a few. Of all the cases I've seen in therapy, those who have a strong spiritual life seem to do the best. This could come through prayer, meditation, connecting with nature or whatever brings your soul in touch with the divine. Recently a hurricane went through the island of Barbuda and I saw on the news that some people tied themselves down to their houses so they wouldn't be swept away. I think sometimes it takes this much determination to remain connected to God, to creation and to the source of everything. How people connect to God is different for everyone. It is challenging in the face of adversity. The bible tells us to be thankful in all circumstances. Recently in the aftermath of Hurricane Harvey there was a news clip of people in a shelter in Houston singing Gospel songs and praising God after everything had just about been taken from them. In Jesus calling I am reminded to thank Jesus for my problems so that I can see Him. That's so counterintuitive. A recent student of mine talked about Deepak Chopra saying that gratitude was the best inflammatory there is. So our go to card may be to say why is this happening to me? To be thankful is another thing. I remember reading Anita Morrjani's book Dying To Be Me. She mentioned that someone told her to keep seeing a Chinese Medicine Practitioner in Hong Kong. She realized after going many times and the hassle that it caused to get there that her intuition told her to go home, light candles, sit, relax and follow her intuition as she looked out her window at the ocean. Sometimes we need to do what our intuition tells us because I believe that the answer is already inside of us in our intuition.

So we can use our ability to connect, to feel, to do, to love, to speak, to follow our intuition and know by being connected to God. We can overcome the storms in our lives in whatever portion we can or we can be overcome by them. Marathons are not easy. Running long distances is physical, emotional, psychological and spiritual. I remember watching a you tube video by Carol Tuttle who said running a marathon is the most spiritual thing she has ever done because it helped her to realize all the limiting beliefs she had about herself. Our life is a marathon and the ability to overcome our challenges I mean to say is already built into us. What is your challenge? Can you use your power to overcome the challenges that face you or will you be overcome? My father overcame two open heart surgeries and took good care of himself. When he got esophageal cancer he did not overcome that challenge. We all have to die sometime. My mother's fear was that she wasn't good enough because she was abandoned when she was three days old. I think her whole life she wondered why she was left because she actually didn't meet her parents. Her challenge was to love herself and not abandon herself. My father always had a can do attitude. He was very poor when he was little. He would tell me that there is no such word as can't.

I've watched Jim Rohn on You Tube. He reminds me of my father. Take charge of the day or the day will take charge of you. Mr. Solar Plexus. He like my father was a person with a can do attitude. This has to do with our decision making and our identity and confidence. When we are faced with storms in life we often find it hard to trust our instincts or our intuition. What my parents taught me was that it is important for me to love me and to believe in myself. Now part of writing is creating. When I create I make better decisions and my identity grows stronger. Creativity can come by playing music and coming up with new ideas to use in therapy. Part of growing is working on myself and then using those tools to bring into therapy. I never ask someone to try something that I don't try myself. We all have storms. There are many parts of us that we can use to overcome the challenges we face. I like to encourage people to use the powers I have mentioned in this chapter to overcome their challenges. Be the storm or be overcome the storm.

Chapter Four

The Enemy versus Challenges, Rights and Abilities

One way I like to look at what people are going through is that I try to be aware of the relationship between the main seven chakras and the enemy, which is the voice in the mind. The voice is accusatory in nature. It is made up of statements you should, you ought, you need, you have, you must, you got to, you're supposed to and you better. On the wall in front of me I can see these statements. This is often the way we talk to ourselves or one another. We can see the presence of the enemy when we are afraid, anxious, worried, judging ourselves, feeling shame, guilt and then judging others in pride. To make it as simple as possible makes it easier for people to hear and for me to explain. So let's look at it like this. The Chakras can be looked at as I am (root), I feel (sacral), I do (solar plexus), I love (heart), I speak (throat), I see (third eye) and I know (crown). There are people who have pointed out that when we judge ourselves or others we feel either pride or self-blame and guilt. When we do this our energy actually goes into a nose dive and the enemy gains power over us. The enemy can be called evil or devil, judge, entity, inner critic or whatever you want to call it. The way we learned to judge ourselves and others comes from wounds in our hearts and minds we experienced growing up.

Essentially, we are often judging others or ourselves so our mind is not on God, but on ourselves and others.

Judgment of ourselves and others affects everything we do. We for example may feel like we don't have the right to be here or the right to feel alive. If we feel this we will feel disconnected, anxious and so that would be based upon a judgment that was passed down unknowingly by parents for example. This in turn becomes a challenge and the challenge is for the person to feel alive, that they do have a right to be here and that they actually have the ability to feel alive. This would be an example of a person having a challenge in this area or root chakra.

Expressing our feelings in a variety of ways is the way we are made. Some people do it more so with music or perhaps words or possibly by being a comedian. There are so many ways that we can express our feelings and be creative. The second or sacral chakra has to do with our feelings, creativity and sexuality. How this begins to be compromised is when we judge ourselves for the feelings we have and end up feeling shame or guilt. We can also judge others for having their own feelings and be prideful without really being aware of it. All that it takes is for someone to think that they should not feel a certain way about a certain thing and then may not express their feelings, or play an instrument or do a painting. Judgement compromises our ability to allow ourselves to create, to express feelings and when this happens our energy becomes bottled up and has to go somewhere. If people stuff their feelings they may do so because it is not safe. Managing our feelings is one thing and parents often wonder when consulting with me about how to build an internal locus of control in their kids so they can experience better emotional regulation.

Language is one way to communicate feelings and music or art are others ways. It is easy to develop judgments about ourselves or others and their feelings. We have the right to feel and life presents everyone with the challenge of expressing our feelings and creativity. Often judgment of self or others hinders this right or ability. So expressing our feelings is a challenge, right and an ability. When people judge and are prideful they are overcooking their ability to express their feelings. If someone cannot manage their anger and they are blowing up all the time this may be because they have learned this by observation as a child. Then there is a power imbalance and they then would not be making good decisions with their feelings or creativity. Therefore if they are afraid and judgment is about fear then their right or ability to express feelings and be creative is compromised. Therefore this part of our body has a challenge. Not allowing ourselves to express our feelings or creativity or not feeling we have a right to will cause a dis ease within our body. Then we will make the decision to not express feelings and too much energy will be contained or held back and can affect our emotional balance or energetic balance.

Making decisions and our power or identity is the next area. When we make decisions out of love for ourselves and others we get the maximum possible outcome for ourselves and others. When we make decisions out of fear we make a less than favorable outcome for ourselves and others. Often we don't look at life like we have the right or ability to make decisions based upon our identity. The challenge here would be to make decisions that benefit us. The third chakra is the Solar Plexus. "I do." "I do what"? So much of our identity is tied up in what we do. You can be a counselor, teacher, drummer, father, husband, author or whatever. My father had a strong solar plexus. He was a can do guy and he did. He was a successful business man, father, husband, grandfather, veteran of World War II guy. He was all can do. When he was young I know he was very poor so it was about what to do to survive and so he was less sensitive about feelings than my mom who was all about love and feelings. My father demonstrated his love by acts of service. It's what he did. He was super responsible and took care of his family very well. So he was challenged at an early age to do. Your challenge is what do I do? Who am I? What are my personal views without judging others or myself? What are my opinions? When we are handing over our power to make decisions, to have our own opinions, to form our identity to someone else, we might as well lay down our sword. If we were taught this while we are growing up we can take our power back from the enemy and determine who we are out of love for God and for ourselves because I believe we are little "I AM's." God's name is "I AM." God knows who He is, has an identity, and has His own judgments. There is where I believe we find our true identity.

Speaking our truth is the next right, challenge, or ability. When we are baby's we don't ask for permission to say our first words or take our first step. Parents don't usually tell kids to not take their first step or say their first word. I don't think baby's are self-conscious about whether or not they should say "mama" or "dada" or to take their first step. What parent wouldn't encourage their kid as they edge around the coffee table or going from one parent to the next with open arms. Where does all this initiative go? Babies are so determined. They are not filled with self-doubt.

I remember the most remarkable example one day doing therapy with a woman who had a raging alcoholic father as a parent. She remembers not her first words or first steps. Who does? One day I asked her a question. She was in the session with her husband whose anger she was afraid of and who often could turn her no into a yes. I could see the answer to whatever question she had coming out of her throat and then she thought about it, froze and said something else. She admitted that she had not said what she really meant. It makes me wonder do we say what we really mean even fifty percent of the time. I know it is important to be tactful and to not intentionally hurt other people. How much of our own truth do we hold back because we don't want to lose another person's love or acceptance?

What happens after all our training by parents, teachers and the like is that we become afraid to be open and honest knowing we have the right to speak our truth and to communicate. We can be creative with our speech and talk about our challenges that we all have. Let's face it we are all challenged by something in our lives. If we are in unsafe, unhealthy or abusive relationships we are then unlikely to express our truths. Speaking our truth is part of living an authentic life and saying what we mean with integrity. I remember a woman telling me that when she judged other people she could feel it in her body and it wasn't good. I've heard it said that when we judge our blood pressure goes up whether we judge ourselves or others. Sounds like God knew what He was talking about when it was written judge not.

Our challenge here is to speak our truth and to say what we mean. We can observe ourselves and see how often we really do this because of fear. We might be afraid of others' disapproval or anger so we keep things inside and suffer. Not speaking our truth is suffering. This is one of our challenges, rights or abilities. Fear is an enemy that can take this power away. Fear is the voice that says we shouldn't say what we mean, we ought to say something else, you need to say something different, you have to say something else, you must, you got to, you're supposed to say something else and you better. This is the enemy who tries to take our power away when we don't speak our truth. When we give into fear, the enemy becomes empowered and the challenge to speak our truth becomes stronger and much more difficult to overcome. If we begin to judge ourselves and believe that we need to keep it in then we will hold back our own truth. If we don't speak our own truth then someone else may try to impose their truth onto us. Not everyone is going to believe exactly the same thing and everyone will have a truth that is specific to them. You can have two Christians and they will each believe different and similar things about God.

I believe that we are given the ability to trust our intuition and that we are being guided by the Holy Spirit. When we do things out of judgment and fear it is challenging to trust this God given inner ability. When we trust our intuition we have peace while following our inner wisdom. We often lose track of when we leave childhood. Do we nurture our inner spirit or are we always looking outside of ourselves for answers. People often look baffled when I ask them what does their intuition tell them? It's nice to be able to watch them look inside themselves and find the answers and they usually don't have much trouble finding it if they just give it a little time. So I try to lead people to the answers that they often already have within themselves. It is extraordinary to see. The enemy or voice in the mind moves the person away from their own spirit and makes them worry about what others think, what others say and tries to get them to believe that the future is going to go bad. This comes from how we were trained when we were little and we end up thinking and believing the same way and do the same things that others do. I try to use this intuition as much as possible and when I do I feel like I am being steered from within. If I start worrying and becoming afraid then I start trusting less and things don't flow as well. Depending on God is about trust one step and day at a time. This is where our intuition comes from if we would let ourselves tune into this. Dependence on God is power not weakness. Weakness is pride and self-pity, two things that are seemingly impossible not to do. God shows us the way out of this.

When we follow our intuition we have peace and when we listen to the voice in the mind that judges we do not have peace. We have doubt. A lady whose son I see in play therapy told me that she saw herself and her son back in the home that they had to leave because of all the drinking and fighting they had experienced. She and her son had to leave and go to safe place and she decided not to be married anymore seeing the situation as unworkable. Her son had been through a lot and had ingested if you will, all that energy. She had sought help herself with her own issues and was challenged with keeping her relationship with her son together because of substance use and domestic violence. She worked on herself and kept taking her son to different therapies be they play, music, occupational and speech. She said the most interesting thing when I was consulting with her. "I kept seeing my son and I back in our home together." That was her intuition and the enemy or voice in the mind kept telling her to do otherwise. She chose the more peaceful option somehow and it materialized. The enemy is the voice we hear in our head that tells us not to follow our intuition and therein lies the challenge, which is to follow our intuition and this is an ability we are born with. Sometimes we need to rest, but the voice in our mind will tell us to do more or our intuition may tell us to use our talents, but the enemy may be telling us not to use our talent and that everything will go bad if we do. Sometimes we become afraid that people will not love us anymore. So, there are things our intuition is telling us, but fear gets in the way and we don't use our ability and ignore what is best for us.

We all have a right to be connected to the divine. This could be very different for many people. It can mean many different things like going to mass, visiting the temple, connecting to nature, praying or meditating just to name a few at least. We are so conditioned to be living according to what is outside of us so our challenge or ability to connect to our spirit can be really hard to focus on. We have been so conditioned by our experiences, parents, teachers and leaders that we are trained to pay more attention to others than we are to ourselves. The enemy is fear and this keeps us from connecting to the divine inside of us. It seems to be that almost everyone has a different way of connecting to the divine. Some pray to Jesus, some listen to spiritual music and such. In my career as a therapist and in my experience the people who get in touch with their spirit seem to be stronger and more resilient than those who don't. The former seem somehow to be able to get through things more and see focusing on God as the bigger picture. The enemy if I may lives in our mind, but God is about the heart. We can follow religious norms and practices daily, weekly or monthly. Somehow we can lose touch with God even in our rituals I believe if it is not what is in the heart. We might judge ourselves and be afraid if we don't pray a certain way like a strict mental curriculum. Then we feel bad if we miss an hour or day if we don't pray. We may judge ourselves. God is everywhere and available all the time. It may be challenging and we may be afraid if we don't say a certain prayer. Our heart is our prayer I believe, the most beautiful prayer. The enemy tells us it should be done this way or that way, but I remember a brother once told me that Jesus wants your heart. Sometimes we can just be saying words so we can repeat prayers or try new ones either way I believe it is what's in our heart that counts. We give the enemy power when we feel like we should, must, have to, better, need to, ought to, got to pray a certain way. Our challenge is to connect to the divine from our heart and this is our right since we were made to glorify God along with the rest of creation. We have the challenge, the right and the ability to connect to God, but when we listen to the enemy in our head it becomes a struggle and drains us.

Chapter Five

Battleship

People snicker when I mention this of course because they hear me say something like "love is a battleship." The first thing that comes to mind is all the troubles they have had or challenges they have faced. Many people are in unhealthy or abusive relationships so it is up to both people to agree to continue the way they are or to change.

I like to use the term battleship because a healthy or strong marriage or relationship can be a powerful thing. A battleship is strong when it works at 100% and has the potential to do many things like cause happiness in one person's life. Battleships don't function as well if threats hit the ship, for example, the Japanese zeros that flew into Navy ships in WWII. When this happened everyone was focusing on the damage, fire and destruction. It is the same with relationships. Three common threats are adultery, addiction and abuse. A relationship cannot survive too well when one of these three run amuck. Adultery divides the energy in the relationship, addiction demands all the energy of a relationship and abuse grows fears like a wildfire. There are other types of threats like emotional affairs at work, too much time at the gym, lousy self-care like too much food or not enough rest, too much time on the internet, too sensitive, not sensitive enough, too much living in the past or future whatever. Just like a virus can corrupt a computer threats can corrupt a battleship.

One day I was doing a play session with a child and they wanted to play Battleship. This is a very slow deliberate game like Bingo. It doesn't have the pop and flash like the video games of today that are super sophisticated so I am a little surprised that kids are even interested in such a slow paced game such as this. However, it is not about playing the slow deliberate game of Battleship. It is about connection. Kids want to play Battleship because they want to connect, which of itself is a construct I use when conducting play therapy with kids and consultation with parents. Kids who connect well with others have a good self-image and are affirmed through their positive interactions with others. If kids don't have a good self-image then they will seek attention in negative ways in order to get attention.

If a person is connecting well to themselves then they will be better off on their side of the relationship. If a person is fearful in nature and feels the need to control the other person, then they may make efforts to control the other person. If a kid is playing the game Battleship in therapy and they don't want to play by the rules then they may casually try to look over the top of the board and see where my ships are, which is a blatant effort to see where they stand in the game. When a person tries to control the other person's side of the board then they may feel like they need to play by their own rules or make up rules as they go along. It is important that relationships or marriages have rules or order in order to sustain itself. No addiction, adultery or abuse is a good start.

So each person has their side of the battleship to tend to. Not being connected to one's self is a threat to the battleship or relationship. What does this mean? Good questions to ask yourself are:

1. Do I feel alive?

2. Do I express my feelings and creativity?

3. What do I do? Am I good at making decisions?

4. Do I love myself?

5. Do I speak my truth?

6. Do I trust my intuition?

7. How am I connected to the Divine?

How we answer these questions will determine how we are handling our side of the ship or our side of the relationship. If we are not grounded and connected to who we are then we may not feel alive. It is not up to the other person to make us feel alive. It is up to us. We may feel great when we are with a loved one, but it is up to us to be connected to ourselves and to God. You can have a church full of 500 people and they will all have a different viewpoint on God. What helps me to stay connected to God is to talk about God or read a devotional about Jesus. It can also be contemplative reading of some mystical text that is inspiring. Being connected to God, your Source, Oneness, the divine, or whatever your faith tradition is, is important. For me, Jesus is God. That is my truth. My point is if we are not grounded in ourselves and not grounded in our spirit or God, our relationship will be affected. Not being grounded is a threat to a relationship.

How we express our feelings and creativity have a significant impact on our marriages or significant relationships. Communication is a key component to a healthy relationship. However, we are all taught to communicate in different ways based upon our family of origin. I have learned that the ways people communicate are assertive, passive, manipulative, passive-aggressive or aggressive. When you look at those different styles only one of them is actually good. Apparently, we did not get the memo. So many relationships fail because we don't have good communication. We end up communicating in ways that work against others and ourselves. Poor communication is a threat every time and it comes in many varieties. If we are not aware or just don't care then it may not go well. It's like each person is at their own gun Tourette and aiming at the threats coming to their side of the ship. It is important to concentrate on your side of the ship or relationship. The idea is to shoot down the threats to the relationship on your side of the ship. Most importantly it is important to shoot them down before they get there. Think of the zeros in World War II. If the person in charge of the guns shot them down before they got to the ship then the threat was averted. There are always threats as long as you are at Sea, as long as you are on the battleship together. If a threat makes its way to the ship without being dealt with ahead of time then it's pretty messy and there is a big pile of flames to deal with. If one person lets in a threat then both will be affected. Having a healthy relationship is a high stakes game because your heart is on the line. When people get hurt or have their hearts broken they may hesitate before getting into another relationship or never get into another relationship. Sometimes people will get into a relationship as a rebound and often miss a lesson that was meant for them. I remember Joel Osteen from Lakewood Church in Houston shared that he loves God, himself and then his family. He knew that his personal and spiritual connection to God was the most important relationship then came himself and his family. I believe if we put God first then other our relationship with ourselves and others will fall into balance. I think this is especially hard for moms. I come from a very big family and my mom was always worrying and stewing about her children. I heard it said that a mother is only as happy as her saddest child.

The fears that people have deep inside themselves can also be threats to the battleship. Suppose someone was abandoned as a child and then they learn about this when they become older and find out they were adopted. Then who their parents are becomes this ever pervasive mystery that haunts them in the form of fear. They may ask questions and wonder if they were not good enough to keep. Maybe they will go out of their way to reassure their own loved ones that they will never abandon them. They may do so to the point of giving too much of their power away by having other people make too many of their decisions for them. When one doesn't feel empowered to make decisions then other people will make decisions for them. We may feel more comfortable having someone else make the decisions so we don't have to be responsible or maybe some people were taught or coerced as children to think this way about themselves. In this regard the question is are we taught to make decisions that bring the best possible outcome for ourselves and others out of love or are we making decisions out of fear, which will not bring us or others the best possible outcome?

How do express love in our relationships and are we expressing love at all? Do we express what is in our hearts or are we playing out scripts that we recorded in childhood? I think it is easy for our unconscious mind to replay what we were observing in our childhood. I wonder if we are expressing love towards ourselves or are we hardly aware of what that means at all? I have asked people for years if they love themselves and it seems too often the most bewildering question I ask when working with people. My mom would tell me to be good to myself. I would always brush this off as some sweet innocent remark and never really absorbed what she was really saying. I took it at face value and was concrete never looking past her words. Missing the message happens often in communication. There have been so many times and so many ways I have heard love the Lord your God with all your heart, mind and soul. And love your neighbor as yourself. I always like to use what I read on myself and then take it to therapy and use it with people I work with. My mother was so loving and was such loving person to everyone she met. I think I saw her loving other people more than I saw her loving herself. My mom did love herself and there is not a doubt in my mind about that. I watched her give her love to all her children and my dad. I don't know how much I saw her love herself because she was always doing for her kids and my dad. My parents had a very loving marriage. My mom loved my dad and all my siblings. It didn't really dawn on me that what she was telling me all those countless times was really to love my neighbor as myself, which means that begins with me. So the more we love ourselves the more we will be able to love others and this will translate to our relationships. This may mean saying no to ourselves in order to undo unhealthy patterns we may be entrenched in and it may mean being able to say no to other people in order to protect ourselves. This may be very difficult, but it will be important if we want to protect the battleship. So, the most important ingredient in the relationship we are in is love and it starts with us. What does

it look like to love ourselves a little more every day and what does
it look like if we do this in our relationships? For me, God comes
first because that is the most important connection we have and
yet it is spiritual. So loving ourselves and being in touch with our
spirit is the most important thing. We need to not forget ourselves
while we are in a relationship and that it is easy to spend all of
our time giving when we still need to give to ourselves. We might
give ourselves time to just be, to create, to work on who we are,
to love ourselves, to say who we are, to trust our intuition and be
connected to our spirit, to God. Just loving ourselves may be our
biggest challenge.

Another important part of the battleship is the idea of speaking our truth. Being true to who we are and speaking our truth
could be our biggest challenge. We may not value ourselves enough
to feel like we can speak our truth or we could be with someone
who it doesn't feel safe to be ourselves with. Speaking our truth
may have been something we were taught not to do in childhood
and then a person may spend much of their life never feeling comfortable with their own truth. In therapy it is challenging for one
to speak their truth and hopefully they feel safe doing so. Usually
there is a fear behind someone not speaking their truth. Maybe
they were afraid of a father who drank too much and raged at the
drop of a hat. Not speaking our truth can be a threat to a relationship by keeping things inside and then later on we will have to deal
with that energy sooner or later because everything is energy. I
remember working with a couple where the wife was asked a question and I could literally watch her throat and recalibrate her answer to one she found safe or acceptable. Later in another session
she was able to say what she really meant. It was one of the most
profound examples of body language I had ever seen in therapy.
There was an imbalance where one was not able to say enough
and where one said too much and could not stop talking about
themselves. What we say and what we don't say can be a threat to a
relationship so this points out how important it is to pay attention
to what we are saying and what we are creating with our words.
Are we speaking with fear or are we speaking with love? How we

handle this question will go a long way towards defining how we treat ourselves and how we are showing up in the relationship.

In the next chapter I will focus on our intuition, which is another key ingredient in having a healthy relationship with our self and with others. Kids follow their intuition naturally, but as they continue to grow and become conditioned they must focus more on external factors like their parents, friends, rules and teachers. It's like we join a herd just going along. It seems to me kids live more and are in tune more with their heart and their intuition until it almost gets trained out of them. I believe as adults we often find ourselves lost and separated from our intuition. Anita Moorjani wrote in Dying to Be Me, she had to live from the inside out. Tuning into our intuition I believe means tuning into our spirit and into our heart. In my experience the people who have appeared to have handled challenges well were those who were in tune with their intuition, heart and spirit. It is just the way we are made and to neglect that part of ourselves will make life more challenging because we can't constantly follow what is outside of us and be at peace.

Ultimately our highest challenge is to be connected to the God. So many times whether in the bible or out of other people's mouths I have heard that God comes first. One of the most meaningful devotions I have ever read was from Jesus calling where we are told to thank Jesus for our problems so we can see Him. That seems so counterintuitive, but I believe this is the most critical factor in maintaining a healthy relationship with our self and with others. The battleship is to be protected from threats and there are many that we will contend with. God declares in the old testament that his name is I AM. Jesus in the new testament said that before Abraham was I AM so for me that makes Jesus God. However, that is my truth and my path and I realize that people are on different paths such as Native Americans being more in touch with spirit or nature, Hinduism, Buddhism, Judaism, Islam and on and on. A cousin once said that it was simple. Love God and love your neighbor he told me. Maybe it's meditation or just nature. Nowhere else is our identity found than in our spirit. I believe that we are little

I AMs. Portions of the divine if you will. The easiest way to love ourselves is to love God first. There is a piece of art in my office that was a pure accident. One day I attended an art therapy seminar at my work and I have always been challenged by art. Meaning I'm not good at it. However, we were instructed to make something that represented something spiritual in our lives. I only had a few minutes to make it at the end of the seminar. So at the end I had made an object that some said looked like a Japanese gate or someone said it looked like a guillotine. Two little pieces of wood lay flat next to each other. Out of each piece of wood came a column. Over the top of both columns was another piece of wood. To explain, each person grounded in God next to each other can hold up the relationship. Pure accident and pure simple. It is a metaphor made out of wood. So our biggest challenge is to keep God in our life, in our relationships because I believe it is the most important ingredient that we are made of.

Chapter Six

Flying without Instruments

I love using the Chakras as a way of explaining how we are built. The third eye chakra is all about our intuition and following what is on the inside as a reference point. So often I run into people who ask my questions about what to do in their particular situations. They are typically bewildered when I turn their questions back on them. To be realistic, there are complicated problems that people bring to therapy and there are many particulars at work if you will. People can have trauma in their background and have significant difficulty in relationships. There are so many experiences that people have had by the time they get to therapy or even if they don't go to therapy. We have been programmed by the people who were in charge of our lives and by all the experiences we have had such as moving, divorce, and being deployed to a foreign land for the military. It's really countless. Our intuition is more of a moment thing. What does your intuition tell you now? Without instruments is another way of saying what other people have told you to do and how to act. What works for someone else may not work for you at all. Why does a compulsive shopper buy things a lot? Why does a frugal person put so much effort into saving? Why does someone get too angry and another remain calm? Some people I believe are more intuitive than others, but I believe this is an ability we all have on all levels. Usually children intuit much better than adults because adults are in their heads with so much thinking and overthinking. I like to think of intuition as the Holy Spirit. We have been trained however to not listen to it. I may be wrong. Usually when I follow my intuition I have peace. When I follow my thoughts that is when fear can set in. Fear constricts everything and we become small as I like to say. Steve Martin the comedian had a routine about let's get small. We get smaller when we don't follow our intuition. Love expands and we are open not closed. So, I believe one of the keys is to be open to our intuition and see what it is telling us to do. It could be something as simple as get something to eat. It seems to be that it is never complicated. It is always clear. When we are little we are not always analyzing different outcomes we just do what comes next and what is in the moment. When we are little we are in our hearts more and not in our head. When we get older and grow up, we are always in our heads. Don't get me wrong. We have things to do like wash the car, pay the bills, plan for a vacation, run all our errands and such. It's like over time we get programmed to be in and stay in our head. We go from our hearts when we are little and somehow we end up in our heads and get lodged in their like a tick. Like a tick we get bloated with thoughts that accumulate over time and we feed on them and can't function.

Our intuition helps us see life from the inside. What do you want? Where do you want your life to go? What does your heart say? I remember a brother of mine said Jesus wants your heart. I remember reading mystical texts that stress that prayers that are most powerful are those from the heart. I like to think my heart is my prayer. Intuition shows us a picture of what is on the inside of us and of what is in our hearts. We all have navigation systems on our phones or cars that tell us where to go and those things are extraordinary. What if though we start following the navigation system on the inside more. Where does that lead us? We are always I believe being guided toward our higher good. For each person that is something different.

So back to people. When people pose a question to me I put them on the spot and ask them the question and the amazing thing is they have the answer almost all the time. If not, we are usually able to guide the issue according to what is in their intuition. Other issues can easily come into play and cloud our intuition, which I believe is really spiritual. Flying without instruments means you do not follow what is outside of you to your destination, you follow what is on the inside of you. You don't go by other people's thoughts or opinions unless it serves you well. If you give your power away and let others make all the decisions for you because you are afraid they will eventually reject you anyway then it is pretty tough to follow your intuition and fly without instruments. If you don't express your feelings or creativity because you think people will call you stupid then you may keep that inside when your intuition is telling you to get it out. Maybe you want to sing. Maybe you want to be a public speaker or weatherman. Whatever. If you are not connected to yourself you will likely go by what other people want from you or prefer. If you don't love yourself and nearly everyone I meet in therapy really doesn't know what loving yourself means, then it will be difficult to follow your intuition because it will be in your nature to not follow your intuition. You might think you are bad or selfish for following your intuition. Think about the way you think and ask yourself who taught you to think that way. The instruments are all the thoughts, opinions, directives, orders, put downs and such that other people have others have put in our heads over the years that have programmed us to be the way we are now. And that is the key word ironically. Now. What is your intuition telling you to do or how is it telling you to be now? Can you fly without instruments? Following our intuition is something we can begin to practice with every choice we are faced with.

I think that people are afraid to follow their intuition because they are afraid that it won't be practical. How can I do all that stuff I have to do today and still stay in touch with my intuition. If you try you can use your intuition in everything you have to do today. You might start off the morning with a run in the park. Some people call it contemplation. I get that. I can be relaxing with a spiritual book and I feel like I am contemplating or I feel very in touch with my spirit. It's like my awareness expands and I feel that is the point I am trying to make. I feel this entire book is written on pure intuition. If we can learn to follow our intuition then we are the ones who become more in charge of our life. Following our intuition is like knowing without asking and truly seeing our own truth. I like to look at it like life is challenging you, God is challenging you. Our intuition is a challenge, our right and our ability as a human being and part of the divinity within us. We can recognize it as something as a benefit to us when we listen to it and see what it shows to us. No one follows their intuition 100% of the time. There is no sense in being hard on our self for not following it more in our life. When we use it, we look back at how we may have not used it in the past and find a message and a lesson there. This can help us in the future. When we allow our self to be in our intuition it's like we are giving a gift to ourselves. The enemy or voice in our mind is our judgment of others and us. This only causes suffering. Following our intuition is a way toward peace. It may be much more different for you if you begin to follow your intuition more and judge yourself less.

This is the part of us that is spiritual and not connected to things, but too what is of value on the inside. Reflection is important to us when we are using our intuition. I think that this can be confusing because people bristle if I mention the word chakra as if it is completely foreign to them, but If I use the word intuition they are completely fine and they typically understand what that is. Following our intuition is to see and to be able to reflect. I notice that in today's very fast paced world, people are working so much and going it seems as fast as possible. There is no slow down, but we need to have this in order to connect with this part of ourselves. It's like the less we pay attention to our intuition the more asleep we are even though it looks like we are on full alert. Maybe we become fixed if we can use this ability more. What is fixed mean? I believe when we are in tune with our intuition we become more disciplined and less reactive to our environment. This doesn't mean that we become robots who are indifferent or react to everything in our environment with massive over sensitivity. It means we are more disciplined and serene. It doesn't mean that we have become a super passive spiritual person who can be trampled on. It means we are bold and quiet and reserved in our approach to life.

On the other hand, it doesn't mean that we are egotistical or arrogant either. We don't have a need to manipulate or be rigid, dogmatic and talk down to others. The balance is we are not lodged in our thoughts and not overcome or constantly dealing with fear. We have a little more charisma if you will and have a vision that we continue to follow steadily as if we are canoeing down a river. We become a master of ourselves instead of being at the mercy of what we think the world wants or what someone else wants thereby giving charge of our lives over to everything and everybody else. Sometimes we have a telepathy wherein we can feel the truth even without words. This is a way to describe really being in touch with our intuition and who we are. As you may see, this allows us to have room to be ourselves instead of being tossed around by everything that is outside of us.

Chapter Seven

Kickdrum

When we have a persona that we wear to work, or church, or home it looks like that is who we are, but this seems to be what people do. They are one way with their parents, another way with people at work or school, another way with their friends. It seems like we are being shape shifters all the time. Maybe that is the way life just is. Maybe the beat of the drum is different depending upon whom we are with. Of course, it is easy to compare to music per se. There are many different types of music and many types of instruments used to play that music. From pop to heavy metal to country to classical. However, I would like to use one instrument as a tool to describe who we are and how we make decisions, which is the bass drum or kickdrum in a drum set. If you hit it really hard it is obviously forceful. Maybe however you are playing along to music that doesn't require that much force, but requires instead more finesse. In heavy metal we can hear the kickdrum easily because it is being hit so hard by the drummer's foot. In jazz it is more subtle, and more about finesse and less about power. So, let me apply this to our decision making.

When we make decisions, we act. Sometimes we make decisions, good ones that reflect a lot of good power and of course sometimes we make decisions that are powerfully bad for us or others. So, when we act it defines in part who we are and what we tell the world about ourselves. Sometimes we may not hit the drum with much umph and we find there is something lacking in our decisionmaking ability. We find that our energy is low and that we are not feeling too good about ourselves. We can function, but it is just kind of like going through the emotions. If you are lacking personal energy and don't feel good about yourself, it could be your drum needs some tuning. Perhaps if you are not feeling good about yourself, you are more self-conscious and this will get in the way of your intuition as I mentioned above and also get in the way of your decision making ability. I'm thinking of it as a human is an electromagnetic conductor of energy and so as energy travels through us things may not flow as well if we are not in a state wherein we can make good decisions. If we are wishy washy in our intuition then when it comes time to make a decision, we will not have much kick in our decision making.

This is when we begin to become more self-conscious and start second guessing ourselves more. I believe this most often happens when people are trying to figure out where they want to go to eat when they are driving around in the car together. I think people do this by the masses. When we are not making the best or cleanest decisions, we begin to become quietly confused and we begin to stew and feel insecure. Here is where our security may be most affected.

Let's take a look at this going the other way. I remember a shaman saying to me all life is about energy and it is seeking to balance itself out. Looking at it this way I wonder if we ever have the right balance much of the time. When our decision making is out of balance going the other way we can become a workaholic and spend too much time at work because we don't know how to be alone with ourselves or with other people. Maybe we resent authority and don't want anyone to tell us what to do therefore we may be rebellious towards authority when it may be in our best interest to follow the words of those who are in charge of us. I don't know many people who don't have a boss in some form or fashion. If we are not feeling good or secure, then it is natural to feel not so good about ourselves. When we are feeling challenged by life to declare our identity, make good decisions and own our own power then we can find ourselves becoming too complex because we are going to be going back and forth between the polarities of feeling good and not so good about who we are. We can become too intellectual and too in our heads because we are thinking so much and over analyzing everything.

What else is happening here? We are beginning to feel powerless when we are challenged with identity and decision making. The more afraid we are, the more controlling we will become so we can believe the illusion that we can control other people and make them do or be who we want them to be. We may feel totally powerless and begin to withdraw because we may not like ourselves. We may therefore not make good decisions with our feelings even and stuff our feelings and then end up exploding into violent outbursts. We may feel that other people are trying to control us so we may become stubborn and hard headed thereby becoming rigid and having a superiority complex. I feel this energy when talking with parents sometimes who have too many expectations, rules and who are very hard on themselves. Thereby we are afraid of being vulnerable. This gets a person into the area of narcissism because they don't feel any healthy validation on the inside of themselves and seek it outside of themselves in the form of grandiosity or omnipotence.

There is nothing wrong with competition. Many of us love sports or had siblings we competed with. I remember having brothers at home growing up who were all older than me and I had to work hard to win at basketball, chess or golf. I don't think I ever won at golf. We can be too competitive however and work against the spirit of collaboration in the work place, in our marriages or families. Out of balance decision making can leave us in a domineering place or position and people may be put off if we are too competitive or rigid. Maybe when we are not making decisions that are benefiting us, we let other people put too much on us and then we become over responsible for their lives such as often happens when there is addiction in a family to use an extreme example. When we are afraid we may try to protect ourselves too much and become greedy and end up having more than enough of something, but also end up being very lonely indeed.

When our decision making is off our self-esteem will be low and we will doubt ourselves often. This happens when we listen to the enemy or judge in our mind. What happens as well is that we are not handling our feelings well in the same way we are not handling our intuition well. What happens then is that we become angry more often because we are not letting our feelings out in a way that is beneficial for us because we let it build up and then we don't listen to our intuition as well. Thereby we become a powder keg and if we do not handle this energy well over a long period of time we will begin to manifest physical symptoms with regard to where the solar plexus is, the part of our body where our decision making, identity and self-esteem come from.

How do we know when we are hitting the kickdrum just right for us? We and our decision making are in balance when we are joyful, feeling good about ourselves and have good self-esteem. We feel strong and we have a healthy feeling of having personal power and we don't try to overpower others or let others overpower us. We feel relaxed most of the time and we are multi skilled because we are not made I believe with one talent, but with many skills or abilities. We can be several things like an athlete, a musician, a doctor, an author or a great communicator.

This is when we love and accept ourselves and we stand up for ourselves more. We become strong and more courageous while feeling worthy of love, kindness and respect. We choose the best for ourselves and express ourselves in a powerful way. We are proud of our achievements while honoring ourselves. We choose to be in healthy relationships and are more genuine and are more in charge of our lives. Appreciating our own strengths, feeling power and feeling free to choose are ways that we become more in touch with our identity. We are at peace with ourselves and are seeking opportunities to grow. We are, by doing these things for ourselves, affirming our own life.

So, your personal power is balanced when you feel a healthy sense of power, when you are self- motivated and decisive while also having a good self-image. You will know you are making good decisions and have personal power when there is more harmony in your life and when your energy is balanced. You may feel more responsible in your life and for your life. When you are hitting your kickdrum just right for you, you will feel more reliable and you will accept yourself more for who you are thereby making it easier to deal with others. This is all part of loving yourself more and is one of the areas we can strengthen in our own lives. So how we hit our kickdrum is our own way of finessing our decisions, owning our power and being more in charge. This is our ability, our right, and our challenge.

Chapter Eight

Be Good to Yourself

This is what my mom said to me on countless occasions. It almost had a near generic feel to it. I wondered why she was saying that to me in the first place and it was the same as reminding me that tomorrow was Friday on Thursday evenings. There was always something in the back of my mind however about being good to myself and what that really meant. I never really knew what it meant and so I just let it be said and then my reply was 'ok I will." She meant it with love though I never even asked what it meant. What does be good to yourself mean? What does it mean to you?

Then around the time I was 48 I began to ponder what it meant. How come I never tried to figure out what it means without dismissing it almost every time? At the time I was starting to begin a journey back to the Catholic Church. When I was growing up I had eleven siblings and as far as I knew I was the only one, and there may be another who had not made first communion and confirmation. I knew that I hadn't as a fact, but it didn't really bother me. I was like most teenagers at the time who as soon as their parents stopped forcing them to go to church, they stopped. I liked going to church okay. I didn't hate it, but when I got to stay home I did. Over time my parents went to their respective church's. My mom was catholic and my father was episcopalian.

The difference to me was the same as comparing Burger King to McDonald's.

I guess the trick is to not brush it over and to really ask ourselves what does it mean to love ourselves? As I had mentioned before it so simple we don't give it much consideration. Somehow at some point shortly after I began to ponder this question I started to bring it up in therapy. It was also at the same time I started to read a lot of the work of Don Miguel Ruiz who I remember stressing so much in the book Mastery of Love that a key to doing well in relationships was to like, accept and love ourselves or things were likely not to go well in relationships. So combine this with my reconnection to the Catholic Church through the RCIA, basically a two year class on the indoctrination into the church, which I got a lot out of. I was always like to put it this way, that Jesus sent his mother after me to pull me into the church and in the words of a nun who taught us at the time, and "she did." Mind you I don't attend church now on a regular basis though I did go to Mass again. I wasn't trying to be Catholic again. I was just trying to have closure because I had been asking the question, how come they didn't confirm me. I was the twelfth child and all I can assume is that they were pretty much tired by the time I came along. So, I did this for myself.

So, this was all coming together at the same time. Going to initiation rights class at church and meeting some really nice people and reading Don Miguel Ruiz books at the same time. Then I started to get it. It just clicked one day and then it truly was an omg moment for me. When I read the Mastery of Love by Don Miguel Ruiz and when I realized that my mom was telling me that I was to love my neighbor as myself all along I began to figure out what that is. Slowly. It wasn't like I suddenly self-actualized at loving myself and was killing it. It was kind of like an archeological dig where I had to gently scrape and brush away what others had told me my whole life and begin to discover what it meant for me to love me. I didn't have to put any effort into trying to get someone else to love me.

What on earth then in the grand scheme of things did this mean for me? For one, it means not giving much attention to what other people think of me. If a person doesn't love, like or accept themselves they will naturally begin to seek validation from sources outside of themselves. We are actually all trained to do this because at a very early age we are focused on what is outside of ourselves because we need to eat, survive and belong. Since we are not able to do these things for ourselves we are built to be programmed from the outside in from our parents, siblings, friends, teachers, religion and so on. At some point we begin to follow our intuition, but we are so young we don't even know we are doing it. We are not aware. So we are built with so many abilities like the ability to connect and feel alive, to feel, to do, to love, to speak, to see with our intuition and to know at a spiritual level. Let's focus on the ability to love in this chapter.

How do we know where the balance is for us in our ability to love? I think when we are not sure of ourselves there is a tendency to be paranoid about what other's think. If we are built to look for validation from outside of ourselves then we can paranoid to a certain degree. Not to a pathological degree mind you in that it often interferes with our ability to function, but it is always right under the surface. If we are not sure of ourselves and don't love, like and accept ourselves for who we are then it is natural to not follow our intuition and to become indecisive. To add to this, we will naturally feel unloved because we believe in the grand scheme of things that love has to come from outside of us. Then what do we do? We look or try even harder to get someone to love us. Mind you I am not thinking in the polarities of black and white. We may already love ourselves to a degree, just maybe not that much. This is when we may become aware that we actually feel unloved when we begin to be aware. Again, we maybe loving ourselves to a degree, but may realize that there is much room to grow.

When this happens, self-pity begins to set in. This comes naturally to us. As soon as we begin to feel unloved or don't get our way we begin to feel sorry for ourselves and as I learned from a shaman I spoke with, our serotonin goes down and our cortisol goes up. Not that I even want to start to get into the research, but that makes a lot of sense. In a book I read by Carver Alan Ames entitled Through the Eyes of Jesus, the point that is made by Jesus on countless occasions in many ways is that the way the evil one traps us is to get us to feel sorry for ourselves or judge others. Our serotonin goes down and our cortisol goes up when we feel self-pity or when we judge ourselves or others. We know that when we do this that our mind is not really on others or God, but only on ourselves so much so that as Don Miguel Ruiz stressed, we become masters at self-pity or judgment. We don't even know we are experts at it. What's the point? The point I gather is that the evil one by training us to wallow in self-pity and in judgment of self and others keeps our mind off of God.

This is when things have gone awry. We realize that we really haven't been loving ourselves for much of our lives because we weren't taught that in the first place. So, then we may have had an entire life of having bad thoughts about ourselves and if we don't love ourselves we will be afraid of letting those thoughts go that don't serve us and our higher good. We won't let go because our identity or persona is caught up into hanging on to things and thoughts about ourselves that we are familiar with. Loving ourselves and letting go of that takes lots of time and effort unless it doesn't. I had a client who was extremely driven and succeeded in her 30s more than most of us do in a lifetime. She did have it all as they would say and was very intelligent and rigid. What that got her was a big house, a big car and a big paycheck. However, there was a precipice. The precipice was her happiness and she always stood on the edge of it.

I had seen her for some time and she always seemed so highly strung. After meandering through what was troubling her and family of origin issues she was out of the picture for a while. Then, she came back. Things had been pretty tough and she tried a little medication to help with her mood. In my opinion, medication on average solves about 30% of a problem. One day she came in and just seemed loose and my intuition was going where is all the rigidity. She is just chill. She looked healthier, her hair was growing out, she was putting on a little weight and was a different person. So, I commented toward the end of the session after she was telling me about some traveling she had done and she said that she just learned to let go of the outcome. She let Jesus take the reins. This didn't mean by any stretch of the imagination that life was totally cake now. She still had things to do and challenges, but there was a significant shift in her presentation. My client was loving herself more and she showed me a video one day of a preacher giving a sermon about Jesus. So her focus wasn't so much on herself and trying so hard as before, but now it was on God more, her spirit and she simply seemed happier and much less complicated. In loving herself more she had let go of the image she had of herself before.

Somehow she had learned to be very critical of herself while growing up and we can do this to ourselves if we are not taught to love ourselves. Some parents will show us how to do this, but most people I have run across have not been taught this. When we are out of balance with loving ourselves we can easily become moody with swings in all directions and I see that in relationships where there is a lot of fear. There is usually one who is very possessive. Being demanding is also another way we are not loving ourselves because we believe we have to be hard on ourselves and then we too will be demanding on others. How we treat ourselves will be how we treat others. We can easily become manic depressive on a high when things are going our way and then really on a low when they are not. The more we love ourselves, the steadier we will be and we will be more resilient when faced with challenges. We become tense when we are trying too hard to love ourselves and we put too much pressure on ourselves.

When we are out of balance while not loving ourselves we are not compassionate with ourselves and we don't accept ourselves. We tend to be lonely and even anti-social. When loving ourselves is out of balance we tend to be insensitive and we become emotionally closed. There is also a danger to not loving yourself in that you may become so passive and sad that you become selfless and have no regard for yourself. I remember a lady at church once said it is dangerous to not love yourself. Wow! What a profound statement. We can become codependent and look to one person whom Irvin Yalom called the ultimate rescuer. No one can be in charge of our happiness as Don Miguel Ruiz puts it. Our happiness is in our hands. When we put our happiness into someone else's hands we are far too overreaching expecting them to fit into an image we have of them instead of accepting them for who they are. We begin by being accepting of ourselves and if we don't it is up to us to change that. If a person puts someone else in charge of their happiness then the resentment will begin to build because no one can do that for another person. Having the most wonderful person in the world in our lives helps a lot, but if we are not making or if we are not doing things to make ourselves happy then we will miss a lot. The kicker is that the other person will not get our best because the world will not get our best when we don't love ourselves. If we do not love ourselves we will become intolerant of others because we simply cannot handle loving our self. No love will go out and none will come in because our heart chakra will be closed. This is what ends up leaving us jealous of what others have and we become overly critical. We become narcissistic because love has to come from the outside.

If we manage to connect to ourselves through love, then we have a pretty good fighting chance of becoming compassionate and accepting while also feeling more love for ourselves and for others. Fulfillment begins to set in and this could be really unfamiliar for most of us. We can become so familiar with not loving ourselves that we feel like a stranger when we do love ourselves. It is as I like to say an unfamiliar good. We begin to be open to love and let love reside in our heart as we deeply and completely love and accept our self. I remember the part of the bible wherein Jesus had said that to enter the kingdom of heaven you had to become like a little child. There is an inner child in all of us that we want and whom we love. When we love our self our life is more in balance and we are more graceful and we love the beauty of nature and the natural world. I believe Einstein thought there was more proof of God in nature than anywhere else.

One way to look at it is to be open and grateful for the challenges that have lead us to loving ourselves more. We feel more unified with creation and we are at peace. So, what my mom had said made a whole lot of sense although I never really saw it how she meant it and I will spend the rest of my life learning it. Leo Buscaglia wrote and lectured about love in his life and he said he would never learn everything there is to learn about love in a single lifetime. However, it begins with us. What is in the way of you loving you at this moment?

Chapter Nine

Word

It's how we define things and how we define who we are. With our words we have the power to create and to destroy. In play therapy however, it's not so much what a child says as it is what they do. Their actions describe their life to me and after seeing them several times I can know more about their life and will be able to understand their parents more when I talk to them. I believe Plato said, "you can discover more about a person in an hour of play than in a year of conversation." So much of therapy is talking with people, but sometimes their body language says it all. I remember again the woman who recalibrated what she wanted to say into what she thought was an acceptable answer. You can literally see the words getting stuck in a person's throat. I remember reading a long time ago that body language conveys the majority of what a person is trying to say.

Play therapy is about mirroring and tracking what the child is doing in the session because everything is energy and I will explore more of that in the next chapter. Sometimes it seems that only does our voice convey meaning or messages, but our body does too. Children don't have the word bank that an adult has, but they are usually more direct, sincere and unedited. For adults, words get the emphasis in communication. I had mentioned before that there are five ways to communicate with words. Those are passive, passive-aggressive, aggressive, manipulative and assertive. Only one of these is good, but we are taught all of them and so people are often challenged to speak their truth. Be impeccable with your word is one of the four agreements Don Miguel Ruiz explored in The Four Agreements.

In the real world, this is hard to find even among the seemingly brightest and most educated. Any family that has experienced addiction will find its communication patterns altered. At any time, a person's communication pattern may be altered due to a loss, a move, trauma or illness to name a few examples. As stated above communication patterns in families where there is addiction will often be altered wherein one person is a victim, one is a rescuer, and perpetrator. One person will take on all these roles meaning that from time to time their communication patterns will shift. People may speak one way at work and another at home.

One way one's word would be altered is if they do not speak their truth for fear of abuse or criticism. So, what happens is that they become inconsistent in speaking their truth and they keep it inside. They may have many thoughts that they are unable to express and they may feel like they are being a coward if they do not speak their truth. This can lead to self-judgment which is never good. They may become unreliable because one minute they say something and the next they say something else. If a person does not feel that they can speak their truth then they may become manipulative in order to get their needs met. I don't know anyone who is impeccable with their word all the time, which is one of the four agreements Don Miguel Ruiz talked about. It depends in large part to how we were trained when we were growing up.

We could take it in the other direction. To speak one's truth excessively could mean the person is self- righteous, arrogant and that they force their opinions on others. Speaking your truth is about balance between knowing when to be public and private about our thoughts. I like to use the metaphor of a butterfly as an example. I learned this early on in my career by working in the area of domestic violence. We all have a public self and a private self. It is important to be able to strike a balance between the two.

Usually we don't see a butterfly unless it is fluttering around and it is usually difficult to notice them when they are being still. When the butterfly wants to be public it flies about and when it wants to be private it folds its wings. So, in the same way, we decide when to be public and when to be private or we decide when and when not to speak our truth. No one wants to know what we are thinking all the time unless its an abusive relationship.

When we speak our truth well we are a good speaker and we become more creative because we are not always recalibrating our answers. We find that we are centered and this is the balance in speaking our truth. We may find that it is easier to be connected to God because it is truth and our truth.

When our lives become stagnant we tend to be obsessive. Obsessively worried about what people say or if we have said too much and we have begun to speak more out of fear than out of love. The more afraid we are the less we will speak our truth, which in turn will also make it harder for us to stand up for ourselves. When we are gossiping we are less speaking our truth and we become closed off and judgmental. We either say nothing at all or say too much.

When we speak our truth, we are more creative because we are being ourselves and everyone is naturally creative. Some are just more in tune with it than others, but we are all born with the ability to create and speak our truth. We speak with more clarity and are more inspired. Sometimes people can be very intellectual when they are speaking their truth, but their words lack emotion. Learning to speak one's truth has an element of emotion to it, but we are taught to communicate the way we do. The good thing is we can change the way we communicate and practice speaking our truth every day. It helps us to be true to ourselves and to be in touch with who we are. Jesus spoke the truth. He didn't mince words and obviously not everyone is going to like what we say every single time. Speaking our truth is a gift of creating that has been given to us and it is a challenge to be able to always speak our truth. If we are with toxic people it may be nearly impossible because someone's safety may be compromised.

Being able to feel free to speak your truth may be something that is just new to you. You may have come from a background of violence or addiction, which stifles our ability to communicate. Sometimes breaking these patterns can be very challenging especially if we have been used to them most of our life. It takes practice. So many times, people come to therapy and they just cry right away because they have been holding so much in for so long.

If a person is more comfort oriented, they want to not be challenged. They may find it easier to not rock the boat so to say and just keep quiet. And people may be used to them not speaking up. If we are more of a comfort person, people may become frustrated with us because we don't, according them say enough. If a person is like this they will be more comfortable with holding their truth in. They may suffer in silence and therefore become accustomed to not saying their truth and ignoring things that they need. If a person does not feel strong enough to speak their truth they agree to have things done for them without having any input. This person may not have been taught to speak their truth therefore they may not think that they have a right to do so. If we are too comfortable to not speak our truth we keep to that because we believe the cons far outweigh the pros and the see saw never moves. When we are on the downside of a see saw it is up to us to push with our legs so that we balance upwards. In the same way when we don't push our words out then we stay in the same position and we don't use our strength, in this case our words. When we are on a see saw we are waiting for the other person to push so we can enjoy the experience. If only one person pushes then the experience is one sided and someone will become frustrated. So if it is safe for you to communicate, then try it a little more than you have been because your truth works against you if you keep it inside.

Alfred Adler wrote much about family psychology and the styles we use to communicate so people have a comfort, pleasing, controlling or superior way of communicating. It helps to describe how speaking one's truth is challenging for each person. We all want comfort in our lives, but I am reminded in the devotional Jesus Calling that it is an illusion to have a trouble free life. So no matter what our tendencies are in communicating and speaking our truth, we will be challenged regardless of who you are. If you only seek comfort and pleasure and to have an easy life while also being pampered, communication will be an issue. In this situation you may seek to avoid stress at all costs and you may not want anyone to put any expectations on you. Working regularly, being self sustaining if possible and being responsible may be something to be avoided. So someone with this communication style is usually slow to motivate because of fears they have.

It is no surprise that others will get irritated and impatient when encountering this person. A person who is comfort oriented may speak their truth more when things are easy going and when they have few demands on them. They have a way of minding their own business and try not to stand out. These are people who are peaceful and get along with most everybody. A person who speaks their truth in this way is usually mellow, empathic and understanding. I know a person who communicates in this way. They don't say much and are very shy and socially phobic and introverted. However, when they speak, they speak with much wisdom and I take note of the wise things they say. I find this remarkable and so it is easy to make the assumption that If someone is a comfort person who is shy and doesn't speak much that they don't know much when in truth they can be wiser than you. The challenge then for this person will be to not underachieve and to not undervalue themselves.

One way to look at it is that people have different intentions when they communicate. If a person has been trained as a child to seek approval from their environment, then their goal when communicating much of the time is to please others and to meet their needs. This means that they were taught to give their power away and what comes along with this dynamic is the fear of rejection while at the same time making themselves responsible for other people's emotions. Usually people are happy at first with someone like this because they are so easy to get along with. Later however, a person may find they're annoyed by demands for approval. A pleasing person I have shared with people is the easiest one to get along with because they are so good at connecting because they are so friendly, helpful, reliable, thoughtful and nice. However, people with a pleasing intention worry more about meeting other people's expectations and they don't think they are allowed to get their needs met. This person may often put themselves of the position between someone else's needs and their own.

The energy of controlling people is different. There is a shift between those who are comfort and pleasing oriented people and those who more control and order oriented. We need people to set the time for meetings, to be the boss and be in charge. People like to be self controlled in their communication of their word and they use their words towards control of themselves, others and situations they may encounter. Everyone's energy is different. When I am around a control person, I tend to tense up more and I put a little more emphasis on how I am speaking my own truth. I still say what I mean, but I notice that I am more careful. Maybe I am feeling their tension and their innate fear of trying not to be humiliated or surprised. When people have a control orientation, they want to control others and their situations. This is an achievement for them and then they are able to avoid humiliation and being out of control.

So then the reaction of others is to feel challenged, a little tense, perhaps even angry or frustrated. This how a control person uses their word and it is just a style neither right or wrong of communicating their word and truth to navigate in the world. The vehicle here is the word and the throat. The challenge then for the control person is to speak their word without feeling tense, frustrated, or angry. The challenge is the dynamic part. If I am with a person who is more control oriented, it helps me to notice the reactions in my body, my energy if you will and then respond to them after I have noticed my own tense energy. The point is that my energy in my body tells me what their communication style is and how they speak their truth so that I can speak my truth in a way that works best for me. So then if I am in the room with a control person, I can allow myself to relax more so that I can actually have a good exchange with them. What I usually notice is that they end up relaxing when they speak and so do I.

Strong leaders are often those who have a control way of communicating their word. My father was a good example of this. He demonstrated organization and always making good use of his time. This doesn't mean that he could never relax. I remember he always made time to relax because he knew that was important as well. He was even organized when he relaxed and somehow made that work. He was productive and made the most of the day and he used his words in assertiveness to make those things happen. Someone once said that he was the most responsible person they have ever known. I have also heard someone say that life itself is a detour. It never, if you will, goes always as planned. When their life is not going as planed then their creativity is challenged. Spontaneity and control don't often go that well together if one is not careful. A control person on a vacation may want the whole thing planned out for the day to day activities where others who are less control oriented will tend to let a little more spontaneity into the day.

The best of the best of the best sir! I remember that line from the movie Men in Black when Will Smith was taking a test. Sometimes I look at people who have achieved so much like long NBA or military careers or both. David Robinson is someone who had, I think an amazing NBA career and prior to that he was an Admiral in the Navy. How the heck do people do that and how do they speak their word. I think about the bible and the word was with God and the word was God. Jesus is referred to as the word. His word is life and peace. As far as I can tell he spoke his truth, was the truth and said exactly what he meant and accomplished more than any other human being. He was an achiever and an out doer.

However, when I encounter superior type parents or people in consultations I feel the more tense energy in the room when they speak their truth. Why is that? From the Adlerian psychology perspective it seems I would feel this way because of the fear that drives this type of person so much. More is a key word here when talking to someone who has a superior way of speaking their word. What is more? More competent and being more right, more useful, more good, more smart and more better than others. There is nothing wrong in self-actualization. When it is driven by an element of fear then it changes the energy of the intention. We are all competitive in different degrees. Some people cannot stand to be outdone by others. I think about college or pro teams that lose a championship and they are so competitive and driven that they come back the next year and win the championship. They are so driven to win and they use their previous defeat as energy to win. I see this time after time in sports. So, what is painful to a person who speaks their truth through the superior filter is the feeling of inferiority. They try so hard and definitely are the type of person who would become most frustrated when things don't go their way or when people don't do what they want. A superior parent will feel like their kids are not living up to their standards. Don't get me wrong. It is not that a superior person is a bad person in any way. It is just that this is the way they were programmed to communicate. Taking the right and wrong away from the concept makes it much easier to deal with. It is easy to judge and get lost in that judgment. They want their kids to do more, the school to do more and they want others to recognize that they are doing more.

So their word is geared in this way. In my experience the parents who are the most frustrated are those who fall into this style of communicating. Pathologically thinking, the caution flag would be when the person is narcissistic and has no empathy for their kids or others and so they see their frustration only. Since the personality parameters of the superior person are many, their kids or others may feel themselves walking on eggshells and watching every step and word they make and say respectively. To take this idea to the other end of the spectrum to the comfort person or parent, there is much more passivity and the risk would be that of dependency and hardly any parameters in energy or communication. From one end to the other we can say the extremes are pampered to pressing. The optimal communication is in the middle like a compass that points to north. Balance in communication often seems to be key in communicating with couples or parents.

When I was seeing a couple in therapy the superior wife was trying to get her comfort husband to speak up much more. Obviously, she was flustered that he wouldn't speak up more. So, the balance was for her to pull back and for him to push his words out more. I understood her frustration because she is the one that was overexpressing with not a lot of results. I understand his fear of unpleasant reactions to him speaking his own truth. There was a big gap in between. What was most poignant was when she bristled at the end of the session and asked, "well aren't you going to give us any homework to do"? I told her no and I wanted her to think about the feeling she had when I told her that for the next two weeks. Superior people simmer under the surface so I wanted her to be aware of that feeling and what that does to her. Another mom was pressing so hard on her kids they were becoming passive aggressive and doing little things to agitate her because she was trying so hard they knew they could. They were really controlling her. Not the other way around. I was just trying to get her to see this. The only way she could see this was to release and let go.

Other people will feel often inadequate around a superior person. They may not feel that they can speak their truth. Speaking one's truth will be most challenged with someone who has a superior way of speaking their own truth. So, it is natural to want to avoid someone who has this way of wanting to speak. The best way to look at this is to think neutrally about a person who speaks their truth in this style or another way to look at it is to be objective. Then realize as much that superior people often are the ones who are the high achievers and who are most socially connected. They seem to know a little bit about everything and they tend to be idealistic. They are the people who try the hardest and who seem to be the most persistent. They seem to never let up and that's good especially if it means well for the person and for others. When it is driven by fear though, the outcomes will not be as good. This is the horse where you would pull back the most on the bridle.

The person who speaks their truth in this way can become overworked, over involved and overwhelmed. This is when many times they end up in therapy because things just don't seem to be going their way. People tend to end up in therapy when there is the occurrence of extremes. So people have many styles of speaking their truth and speaking ones truth is an ability, right and challenge. We create with our word. This is our God given right. We have all been taught to speak our truth in ways that don't always serve us in the best way. Learning how to fine tune our word is an art form and we are always in school. When we speak out of fear the outcomes don't seem to have the best benefit for everyone. When we speak out of love there seems to be a greater benefit for everyone. Love expands truth and fear constricts the truth and each person has their own truth.

Chapter Ten

Energy

When I was a little kid they said God was everywhere. They said the same thing about Santa Claus. Of course, the first question that comes to mind is how is that possible. Now they say that energy is everywhere. God is all of the places including where we are and where we are not. We naturally tend to think of energy as something we have a lot of or not a lot of. As I get older, my conscience or instinct is to conserve or make the best use of my energy as I can. So sleep is something I use to stock up on my energy and I want to use it wisely. When we are very young, we have so much energy we throw it around wildly like cash. Then as the years add up, we start to conserve our energy and if we don't then life will tell us somehow to slow down and make better use of it. We can say we like the energy of the room or the energy of the person we were with. Everyone has vibes. In fact, I read recently that even our DNA vibrates. The sun and the earth vibrate. So it's not really a shocker to know that we vibrate. There are all kinds of ways to describe this energy.

It seems to me that there are mainly two groups of people. The first one believes that God and us are separate and that we are not woven so to speak into the existence of God. God exists apart from us such as in modern religion. The other group thinks that everything in existence is part of God and that God is in everything. So we are one with God and everything that exists or are we apart from God.

Both paradigms are equally fascinating, but for now for me I will choose the first paradigm, but that doesn't matter here. We can think we are inherently good or say we are born into sin. I think we are born good and then we consciously and unconsciously become corrupted by the world, those who raise us and by life.

You can call it energy, life, chi, chakras, spirit and all kinds of things. Because of modern science like quantum physics, it has become mind blowing. So much so now that it is not uncommon for people to talk about science and religion merging and that science is finally catching up to religion. Balancing our energy is no easy task or is it? I realize the hospitals are full of people who are sick and if they knew of a way to heal themselves they would. I believe that we are learning to heal ourselves more by the information we are discovering. What is our energy like when it is balanced and out of balance. Some people can feel immense peace in the midst of a physical or spiritual storm while others are freaking out. One could say a balanced life could generally be described in the following manner: when a person is centered, secure and personally safe while also being grounded. Perhaps they are a person who feels totally alive, is in good health, who trusts and feels vitality in their life while being prosperous as well.

One could continue to describe a balanced person as patient, enduring, creative and willing to change while nurturing one's self as well. They may feel powerful, motivated and decisive while also maintaining a good self-image. Their relationships would be balanced, they would have good energy and they would be responsible and reliable. So far this person sounds like they're doing pretty good huh? Well that's not all. Let's say they are compassionate, accepting of others, fulfilled in their life, lovable of self, others and open to love. They would be a good communicator and express themselves with creativity while also speaking their feelings with inspiration and clarity.

In addition to all that, they would be intuitive, intellectual, visual, imaginative and come at life from a higher perspective.

Finally, they would be universally conscious, no fear, open to the divine, enlightened and having meaning to their life. Do you know anyone who is like this? I don't and I have never met someone who is fully balanced. Can you imagine being this person every day. I've seen people in my life who seem like they have the sweet life or the charmed life as they say. Where have I seen these people? In church. Wait, if they were perfect then what are they doing at church? People are going to church because they are suffering not because they want to brag about how well they are dominating life. They are looking for something more, they are looking for a connection with the divine, or they are desperate, or they are forced or they want to feel spiritually safe.

Once during my career, I did some counseling at a church when I was between jobs and this was a church that was affluent. Nice cars and clothes were everywhere. Most importantly, there were a lot of nice people there too. Many of them were going through very painful challenging times. So, it is easy to believe that those who look good or who have nice things don't have it difficult. What I mean to say is no one is perfect and it seems like everyone is going through something. It's never cake all the time for anyone.

I really believe that if our parents do not deal with their own fears by the time they have us and are raising us, then we inherit their fears. It could be said sins of the fathers are visited upon subsequent generations. It makes the most sense to me that we take on our parents' wounds if they didn't deal with them. We live in a completely different era when people are now much more informed about the human being and how we function spiritually, emotionally and physically. I don't know if people back in the day when the day was, were working on their emotional wounds. So, if your parents didn't deal with their wounds, then you will deal with them in some way. If you had parents who somehow didn't deal with their wounds or fears of abandonment and not having or being enough, then you will deal with that energy. To take it a step further, I believe it will manifest itself into disease. This is not to say that two year old children who get cancer are bad. I am not speaking in absolutes.

There are so many different ways to look at this. Usually I don't like to look at things in black and white. In the Mastery of Love by Don Miguel Ruiz there is the track of love and the track of fear. Beyond this I remember someone once saying that all that there is in the world is love and the absence of love. I believe that the best place to start is the energy that we feel. We are conduits of energy as energy goes through us such as when we are in a thunderstorm. We can have storms outside of us or we can have storms on the inside of us that no one else can see. There are many different experiences that people have in their families growing up. If there is a lot of criticism then that kind of energy is expressed, absorbed and stored in the body. When we are criticized and take it personally we do it because most of the time we don't know that it is usually another person's energy that they are trying to send to us and get rid of. Constructive criticism is a different thing altogether. If we get criticized a lot as a child then we are not accepting our self and our energy declines. We go through many changes in our lives and alongside those changes such as moving, death, divorce and other changes we may find that we are criticizing ourselves for whatever reason. My point is that we are still creating energy if we criticize ourselves. Any change we go through will create negative energy if we criticize ourselves. And let's face it. We will be going through changes our whole lives. Approving of and accepting our feelings allows us to have more positive feelings.

Sometimes we see so much terrorism on the television, but many times we terrorize ourselves with our own mind. I believe it is very often possible to change what we are thinking. It is easy to scare ourselves with our thoughts and to forget that we can have a more pleasurable image to think about. Different things trend in therapy in my experience. One of the things that I have seen or heard the most is the idea that the couples who do the best are those that show kindness and generosity. In my book, that begins with the self. If you are a pleaser and you are kind and generous to others only then it won't work for long. Being kind and generous with one's self is the beginning of it. What if you never thought this way? Think of the person that you love the most and treat yourself like you treat them.

How could you praise yourself? We are programmed to judge and we can often be critical of our thoughts. How can we love ourselves and offend ourselves at the same time? I don't see that as possible. Yourself and your thoughts are two different things. You are pure energy. You have the power to change that energy in many ways and you might have thoughts that don't serve you or that you don't like. You can observe your thoughts and see what they are teaching you. When you criticize yourself you change your energy and your inner spirit breaks down. Praise and encouragement bring it back up. So it is important to find ways to support yourself. It might be spending time alone with God, going for a walk, sitting outside, listening to music, reaching out to friends or family. It is a strength to ask for help not a weakness. We all need help. In Jesus Calling we are reminded that we need Him at every moment and in the book The Prayer of Jabez we are reminded that when we are depending on God we are strong because we are living by faith. When I was a new intern twenty one years ago I didn't want to ask for any help and I tried to fit everyone into my object relations theoretical box. Object relations was where it was at. Sooner more than later I had a really difficult client. The tiger by the tail. I didn't have all the answers and I needed some grounding so in our group supervision I reached out for answers. That was a turning point and empowering for me because I received some good and sensible answers.

I learned that wherever there is a negative with us, there is a need. Take your criticisms and judgments and turn that negative around into a need. This way we can embrace what we need and change our energy at the same time. Let that negative be your teacher and not your enemy. Negatives are a disguise for a need. Without knowing it, we create negative thoughts because of a need, that we didn't know how to feel. We can develop new patterns of meeting our needs and our energy changes. Our body is as

a doctor once told me an incredible thing. It is easy to judge ourselves and criticize ourselves. I equate this to vandalizing a temple
and that is not what the temple is for. What do our bodies need
to have optimal vitality and energy? Is it sunshine, exercise, rest,
calm, jogging or playing with our pet? I don't do the same exercises
now that I did in my 20's. I am much more aware that my energy,
time, and health are becoming ever so valuable now. When we are
young we say "I'll never die" and when we become older we say
"don't die." Forgive yourself. Pride and self-pity are your enemies.

Life looks to balance itself out. Are we not born with the right
for health and happiness that is open to everyone? Theories, science, religion and philosophy are some ways that people search
for a practical way to understand and live life. I have never met
two people whose beliefs are exactly the same and yet I believe we
have one Creator. God is diverse and One at the same time. I once
heard a very wise man say that life seeks to balance itself out and
that you cannot have more north than south east than west. The
idea of Yin and Yang is energy perceived in two states that I find
fascinating. Yin is being formless and dispersed and Yang is that
of condensation and having form. Formless objects can transform
into objects with form and objects can revert to being formless.
How can this apply to everyday life? How is all this energy seeking
to balance itself out? This energy is coexisting and complimenting
each other. These energies compose and contain each other and
are actually dependent on each other so it is like wise man said in
that you cannot have more north than south than east and west.

One thing that I thought about in regards to energy is that
the parents' wounds are the kids energy. Sometimes I think about
ideas from books by Rasha or Michael Singer that life seeks to
crash into our fears so that we can release wounds and fears. Our
lives are so fast now. Because of technology and the pace of life, it
seems that it is harder to pay attention. Technology pulls us away
from nature. Nature is simplicity and as Leonardo Da Vinci stated,
"simplicity is the ultimate sophistication." When I was little I did
not think about time especially when I was in grade school. When
I did I imagined myself being a senior in high school and thought

that was old. Life was so slow. It took forever for a week to go by much less a year. Now in my fifties I am very aware of time and energy. A thought about something I read in Jesus Calling by Sarah Young. The idea is that Jesus is telling us that time and energy are our most valuable commodities. Weeks go by now almost as fast as a falling star. The hours are shorter. When we are young we run into things and don't care. I am getting older mind you though I don't think I am old yet. Now however when we run into things we go to physical therapy so we can get our balance and strength back. Life seeks to balance itself out.

So, then what is important? Really? Do we have purpose and meaning? Are we fulfilled or are there things left undone? Again, in Jesus Calling I am encouraged to live in the moment. Someone once said that they find themselves living between two crosses. The cross of the past and the cross of the future. One challenge in doing therapy is that I love to read a lot and I am in my head analyzing things. The challenge is to get out of my head. Walking with my wife in nature I am constantly reminded to get out of my head and see the countless miracles before me in the sound of bugs, trees, deer, sky, water, flowers and such. Clutter and complications are the barnacles of therapy. Because of their experiences in life people become so full of clutter in their minds and complications in their lives. I think part of the reason I stay in my head is that my mind is trying to sort all that out. It's impossible. I am reminded by a client who said after giving me a Buddha statue that "if you really love yourself, you won't do anything to hurt anyone else." And an article about marriage emphasized that kindness and generosity are the things that make the master couple. That is balance. That is Zen. That is simplicity. That is living in the moment. We are masters at mucking it up and complicating it. God is trying to show us the better way.

In paying attention to therapy, I think of all the crime shows that are so sophisticated. They always find or stalk the trail and it usually has something to do with money. So, they stalk the money trail. In therapy, I feel like I am always stalking the fear trail in each person. There in a person's fear will lie their challenge. The challenge I see as the biggest is for people to love themselves and when I ask people if they love themselves they are actually confused or bewildered by what that means to them. The ultimate challenge is not to let fear be our enemy, but as a wise man said to let it be our teacher. So, in that way we don't run from it we instead learn from what it is teaching us and we can take our power back instead of it being siphoned by our fears.

We all have habits like getting up in the morning, brushing our teeth, going to work and so on. Habits we don't have control over become addictions and then our life becomes controlled by that. Our energy becomes out of balance and for years our energy can be flagging. Even as a nation we seem so out of balance now because there is so much addiction to alcohol, drugs, money, technology, people and so on. I believe that reconnecting with our spirit is the single most important component of healing in our lives. It takes practice. Each day set aside time for what feels right for you to reconnect to your spirit. Whether it be meditation, yoga, prayer, being in nature, working your steps, working out, reading, singing or whatever. Do that. To make time for devotion every day at work or home is important. It's like plugging myself into the divine.

One thing I have changed at work was that I play healing music at low volume when I am doing therapy. I had a surgery and in my recovery, while I was out of work I listened to music on You Tube. Not music in the sense we have listened to our whole lives. I listened music at different frequencies blended together. I found it soothing, healing and centering. Since then I have been playing music all day long at work at low volume. Nobody minds. People say it is so relaxing. I believe music has the power to heal and we can use it to heal and restore our energy and the balance thereof.

Our energy involves self-healing, emotional well-being, vitality, creativity and personal growth. It goes back to what my mom told me. Be good to yourself. Anita Moorjani said "your mission is to be you." Toward the end of her life my mom told one of my brothers that she was not afraid to die. What a poignant moment for her, for me and for life. Here was the most loving person you could know loving themselves by not being afraid to die. A lifetime achievement. Be you. Love you. Let fear be your teacher. There is only love. Fear is the absence of love. I have heard that love is the highest form of vibration. Loving ourselves is our highest priority and we may need different things at different times and restoring balance in our lives may require different actions or in-actions. Whether it is gardening or hiking there are many things that would help restore balance to our lives. Creative expression and sunbathing might help for some while pampering yourself are just as important as singing. Dreaming of what you want to do could be important for others whether you are 15 or 50 or saying a rosary could be important ways to create balance in the day and in ourselves.

Chapter Eleven

Barnacles

Barnacles are found underneath the boats and they become part of the boat. We are always having things projected onto us even since childhood. Our parents each have their own mental makeup and how often are parents really aware or conscious of what they are doing and the intent behind their consciousness? Life gets in the way so we are not always paying immense attention to what we are doing. We go through childhood and people whether they be parents, siblings, peers, teachers and the like project their thoughts and emotions onto us, their own consciousness and intent. We do the same. We project what is inside of us onto other people and we are a planet of projectors always sending what is inside of us out. There is no way not to do it. You can only communicate what you know, or what you assume, or what you think and then others do that to you. In therapy, the therapist gets a sliver what that particular client has gone through. Imagine if you will a person taking a paint brush and splattering paint in the therapy office. Instead of it being paint, it comes in the form of thoughts, words, feelings or cumulatively speaking, energetic splatter.

Over the course of a career whether it be twenty or forty years of doing therapy, we collect that energy, that collection of thoughts, emotions and experiences and each of those experiences becomes a part of who we are like barnacles on a boat. Barnacles are very tough to scrape off and become a big part of the boat, that part that you don't see. In the same manner our experiences with clients become barnacles on their boat and theirs on our boats.

Raising self-awareness is part of doing therapy as well as understanding our role in our own experiences. Someone thanked me for bringing them back to reality. I don't really know what that means more than somehow they have been able to connect to the spiritual center inside of them and they were very aware of two paths that were set before them. There is the path that feels right for them with God and a path of self-destruction.

And vibes! What about vibes man? We've been receiving vibes and sending vibrations our whole life. People can tune into vibes more than ever and therapist's take on people's painful vibes throughout the course of their career because most of the time people are not coming to therapy to brag. I have been familiar with the research of Masaru Emoto who was a scientist who studied visual changes in molecular changes in water. So when people spoke loving words there was a resonance when the water was frozen and it came out like beautiful snowflakes and when water was exposed to negative thoughts through words the shapes of the snowflakes were asymmetrical and dull in appearance. What this means for us or us as therapists is that we are creating our reality with thoughts and feelings and when we do therapy we are absorbing things that have been predominantly negative in life. So you could say that therapists are taking on bad vibrations while also trying to change the energy of the people they are working with. Self-care is very important for therapists and becomes much more so as we age. Knowing when to refuel and knowing how is vital for someone who is taking on someone else's pain. So consciousness and intent become paramount to self-care.

Everything is vibrating all the time. Even if we don't see. We are vibrating, the sun is vibrating, the earth and everything in nature. Sounds, cells, colors and food even vibrate. All day long in therapy I listen to music at different frequencies that is soothing. Gotta keep those good vibrations happening from the Beach Boys is good advice. I believe sound will be used more in the future for healing and believe that it has helped my body and health to recover from surgery and from hip and bone injuries. Sound can be found to lower blood pressure and heart rate. I am very thankful that I have had a job wherein I can play background music throughout the day and so many times people have shared that it is so relaxing in my office. Could sound therapy in the future boost memory, boost immune function and decrease depression? The therapy that I have done has mostly been traditional even though what I find in most recent history is that I am most comfortable using a combination of Christian, Native American and Hindu approaches. In general I try to feel what the energy is like and find my way to answers with the client. The things I mentioned above I use on myself because I do that before I use them on other people. To put it all simply: Staying in touch with my spirit and God, seeing what my challenges are and keeping life simple are the things I try to achieve.

People can easily become jaded or burned out if they do not take care of their energy. Therapy is such a market driven endeavor. Health insurance companies are often limited in what they will reimburse for and there are some with great benefits. So being a therapist is being part clinician and part business person. Managing all that and dealing with people and their issues is challenging. Barnacles are all the things that we have taken on from our clients over the years. It goes with the territory and it becomes part of who we are. Sound can create disharmonious vibrations in the body and it can create harmonious vibrations. Modern medicine is fantastic. I would like us to see ways in which we can broaden our ability to prevent disease and take our health into our own hands before things get out of hand and we rely only on treatment.

I remember being a graduate student and seeing the psychology section in book stores. It was enormous up and down one really long book shelf aisle. Now it is tiny. Now because of the internet people are educating themselves more than ever and are smarter than ever because of technology. The whole idea behind sound therapy is to create the optimal environment for the cells and the body to begin to heal itself. Musical octaves and octaves of our electromagnetic system are similar and have corresponding colors that represent the different chakras. This paradigm has proved useful in therapy because it helps with people's abilities, rights and challenges. It helps me to see what area of a person is most challenging to them at the time. So when therapists accumulate a lot of barnacles, something is naturally going to be of balance.

Self-awareness, consciousness and intent and the increase thereof may help us go a long way in the managing of our lives. Discovering these different ways of approaching our health and well-being may go a long way towards removing some of the barnacles. Everyone has their own way of approaching what they need. It is easy to become jaded and burned out in this career so self-care is paramount to our health as well as balance. Sometimes it's easy to let ourselves go and that as much as we take care of other people it is important to continue to take care of ourselves and our health as much as possible.

It's easy to stop pushing and to just drift and not take care of ourselves. Perhaps we get stuck in roles, jobs, relationships and spiritually as well. We take on so much of other's stuff and forget to pay attention to our own. Where is your sacred space? Is your desk your altar? Is it at church, adoration of the Blessed Sacrament or at the Temple? Mine is outside. Just now I went outside and the way the sun feels on the first day of spring is my sacred space. I feel warm, well, more alive and I can feel it in my bones and maybe a few barnacles come off. Our barnacles will always point to a need eventually. Maybe it is to disconnect and not talk about another problem and maybe it is to feed yourself silence and pay more attention to being connected to yourself and your intuition or spirit because you can't find the answers anywhere else.

It is easy to get stuck. You can be doing the same thing for 20 years then the passion for it goes away or maybe it drains you. I think in the present day we are expected to go to school, to grow up, to go to school some more and do something for the rest of our lives and then get a watch and die. When I look back in recent history I see people were scientists, botanists, mathematicians, inventors and writers. It seems like our society is more about doing one thing and having a career at it. What if you want to do many things? The thing about the barnacles is that you can get so used to being there for other people that you are no longer are there for yourself and fall into a repetitious existence. What makes you feel alive? If there is an accumulation of barnacles and they are weighing your boat down then it may be time to do something different. Whenever we feel weighed down that is a negative and when there is a negative there is a need. What is your need? Do you need to connect to yourself, to life, to your feelings or creativity, to your own power or identity, to your truth, to your wisdom or to your spirit? Life is challenging you to meet that need. We are human and we can only take on so much and then we can break. Our body will tell us "hey buddy! Now do I have your attention." Unattended to needs manifest in our body in some sort of illness and then we are forced to listen.

Not only do we have our own barnacles to deal with, we have other people's too. The world will take all your energy if you let it. If you never say no you end up being worn out. We cannot say no all the time. However we need to be able to say no when we can and when we need to. Perhaps the answer is that we need different things at different stages of our lives. Maybe in young adulthood we wonder what and why we keep getting things wrong or the higher ground response would be what is the lesson that I have not learned yet?. It seems to me that life is like one of those orange cones you see in a parking lot. Imagine that you lay that orange cone on its side. Now the big end is where you come into this life. It is a very wide opening because life seems endless while time and energy do not really come into play. There is an opening at the other end and that is a narrow opening. The closer you get to it the closer the sides get to you. Your finiteness is closing in on you. The hours are like windows that get smaller and smaller. When you are half way through the cone, you begin to notice the sides more in that you are more aware of people around you dying or getting sick, that you are in the middle or past the middle of your life and realize that what is left. Time and energy are your most precious commodities as is mentioned in the book Jesus Calling.

Time spent ignoring your spirit is a waste of time. So if we are half way through the cone or more than halfway, how do we want our lives to go? Now some people die young and leave before their time so to speak so this brings the average down. What brings the average up?

I remember walking with my wife in the park one day and I out of my own self-importance stopped two ladies who were twins and who seemed to be in their 80s. I said "hello" and then out of my curiosity asked, "I just wanted to know what keeps you going?." Only one of them turned to me as we were walking past each other and said "just keep moving." That was about the third time I had heard that. So, if you can keep moving, move. I feel blessed just to not be in the hospital. Part of balancing taking on these barnacles in your life and in the life of others is to enjoy and be thankful for the simple blessings that are coming our way every day. I live in the part of the country where it is warm most of the year. Sometimes really hot! I have a shirt that says "Nature-Cheaper than Therapy." Psychotherapy is great when it works, don't get me wrong. However listening to and being in nature is more healing. Thank God for people who even want to listen to me and are interested in what I have to say. Sometimes we need to hear and sometimes we need to be heard.

We are not just a palette where upon someone throws their energy. We participate too in that exchange. The metaphor of the barnacles is that they weigh the boat down. Our bodies' record everything we experience so then it will be up to us to manage all that energy in the form of woes that people give us and that we listen to. People are positive in therapy. Don't get me wrong. Often times they like to talk about current events, something they did or handled well or just about some simple things in life. Sometimes the therapist is the heaviest person in the room energetically speaking. We live in such a loud and fast society. It's really important to be able to tune into ourselves. Technology is so sophisticated and is always pining for our attention because it can do fascinating things, but sometimes life needs to be about silence and our spirit. That is why I so often put questions back on people because I think most of the time they already have the answers. We freak out when we don't get a Wi-Fi connection though it doesn't bother us to be disconnected from ourselves. Half of my life at least I believe didn't even have the internet. Knowledge has increased. We can educate ourselves much more quickly than ever before. Learning to tune into what we need as a person does not require technology.

Our body is the boat the barnacles attach to. Our body is ours for our entire life. Not only do the people who come to see us have lessons to learn. We do as well. It is counterintuitive to look at mistakes as lessons in our lives because we are programmed to judge ourselves and each other. It seems as though unconsciously we loop and keep repeating things that work against our better nature. Maybe we dismiss ourselves or give our power away. For our whole lives we get to live only in the moment. There is no future or past. Did you ever notice that subtlety of life? There is only now. So there is always here and now, but we never live in there or then. Only in our minds. All those experiences form all those barnacles we accumulate over the years. How you handle taking care of all the energy is up to you. It will mean different things to different people. What about a pastor or a priest who is like one therapist for the whole flock. I believe if we follow our intuition that it can lead us to the answer. It is in our nature to pay attention to problems and ignore them because we move on with other things. However, we will remember them again.

You cannot be anyone else in life. You can become a better you. Challenges are different for everyone. Recently I did a workplace survey with a local agency. I asked them to rate statements based upon their rights, challenges and abilities. There are only seven statements to rate in all. What I found was that the helping professionals are very good at being creative and expressing their feelings. The irony was is that they were challenged at being connected to themselves mind, body and spirit and on the whole they did not speak their truth as a group. So as a whole they will be better equipped to help others if as a whole and individually when they can connect to themselves and be and feel able to speak their truth more. It is also a matter of finding out what feeds us. Is it intellectual conversations? That may be rejuvenating for some and draining for others. Some people may be energized by being around others while others may refuel by spending time alone in nature. Sometimes people make large moves towards balancing themselves such as moving to a different town or different part of the country while others make career changes because they feel like they have gotten as much out of their career as they can get.

When clinicians feel the weight of all those barnacles they can be proactive in big or small ways in order to create some joy in their lives. Barnacles weigh us down. Joy lifts us up. I once heard someone say they knew a therapist who was giving up their career because they were tired of sitting across from crazy people all the time. I go back to time and energy. As we get older we have less time and less energy. Finding peace in our way is important. Perhaps we need to be more creative by singing or painting. The demand on our energy may be sapping us and we don't always realize that we are taking more in from others than we are giving to ourselves. I see this with therapists who have been in the field a long time. They do more to conserve their energy.

Being a therapist is part of the experience of ever becoming who we are. In order to keep it interesting I can attend continuing education events that are always a learning opportunity. That however is not always the best way I have learned. I don't really feel like I remember all that much about what I learned in school. I like and love the schools I went to. I feel like I really learned the most from the books I chose to read after graduate school and after getting a master's degree. So my interests have traveled from the work of Victor Frankl and Irvin Yalom and onward through psychoanalysis and object relations. Then I learned about personality disorders and trauma in children and adults. When I began my career my internship was in domestic violence so it was baptism by fire because it was such an intense population on all levels to deal with. At one point I began to read a lot of books in Christian mysticism. I never turned back after that because everything became spiritual. Books by Maria Valtorta, Sister Faustina and Catherine Emmerich were a few mystics who had encounters with

Jesus and sometimes his mother Mary. God knows I love to read so He gave me some great material. I love the work by Don Miguel Ruiz also and the Toltec wisdom he uses. Now what I find most interesting are the devotionals from Jesus calling, the chakras and an approach called stalking the enemy, which seems to be Native American in its origins and from Don Miguel Ruiz as well. I always use material on myself before I bring it into therapy to use with clients because I want to know what it feels like to experience each of those approaches.

Sometimes people can go through years of therapy, but it may be a single sentence that stands out in our mind that helps us. My mom always said to be good to yourself. So I am learning as much as ever the importance of loving myself every day. My dad would say there is no such word as can't. So my parents' messages for my life was to love myself and to know that I can. When I was very young I met only one of my grandparents. He told my mom privately that I would make it. I don' t really know what he meant by that. I have been doing therapy for more than 21 years at this point. Did I make it twenty one years ago when I became a therapist? I surprised myself because I was always such a lousy student. Somehow I managed to get past high school and into college on fumes academically speaking. What is making it? Do you just get to a level and top off the richest man in the world sort of thing. Now what? How do you define success? Financial independence? Raising your kids properly? Becoming involved at the church?

I believe that we are ever defining ourselves every day. If someone does something for twenty years then they chose to do that thing for twenty years because they love it, because they had to pay the bills, because they thought they were supposed to do what they are doing, because they didn't follow their passion, because they were afraid they would starve if they followed their dreams and on and on. A long time ago I believe God told me in my spirit to become a therapist when I was asking Him what to do because I was in my late 20's and just didn't know what to do. He reminded me that people used to come up to me in high school and talk to me about their problems out of the blue and I would wonder why they would do that. I believe God was telling me that it was a natural thing for me. So was playing Frisbee although no one would pay me to do that. Being a therapist as I would say has been cool. It has been emotionally draining and now physically too. That is the way it is with whatever you do. You give yourself to that thing that you do it will demand your energy whether you are an NBA star or a policeman.

If I think about what I love it is nature, books and music. The sunshine and the greenery of outdoors is replenishing. Books are fascinating because you create the pictures in your mind when you are reading a book and music just goes off in all directions and there is something for everybody. How can you do what brings you joy and live? What you love to do there will be a demand for it. Whether you want to be a dentist or work at the zoo. Focus not on the things that you afraid of. Instead focus on what it is you want because what you focus on becomes bigger in your life. I heard a wise man say to share the medicine. Maybe your medicine is your humor, voice, counseling, wisdom, creativity, love, truth, connection to who you are, your connection with God and so on.

So then let us find the greatest comfort in being kind to ourselves and others. Our biggest stumbling blocks are those things we are afraid of and a wise man said let your fears be your teacher. We all like to be appreciated so who is it you can appreciate now in your life and will you show it? Being bitter is easy and familiar and it will be challenging to throw it aside, but it is meaningless nonetheless. Being afraid and judging ourselves and others gets in the way of clear thinking, a clean heart and just being. There is nothing more powerful than love, which I hear is the highest form of vibration. God is love. Nothing comes close to being more powerful than our Creator. It is painful to worry and then we get caught up in ourselves and become afraid while fear muddles our thinking. In Jesus Calling the other day the scripture was paraphrased to say that God does not have voices of accusation. They are not from Him. The enemy is the accuser of the brethren. Attitude and cheerfulness can go a long way. Maintaining a joyful attitude is challenging while pride and self-pity are the pitfalls of the human condition. We, like little children, want someone to understand us, to hear us and to care. Life forces us to keep moving forward even if we are standing still we will have to participate in life in some fashion. Loneliness aches and can be crippling. Sometimes we can help those who are lonely. Our greatest problem is our self and when we are preoccupied with our self, we are prideful and engage in self-pity. It seems like we all need reassurance at different times and often because that is human nature. One could say the saddest feeling is rejection. God loves us just the way we are. It is unconditional. Do what brings you joy and get to know yourself as much as you can while you are here. Our life is the accumulation of millions of moments.

The barnacles of other's lives have in part become mine because that is the nature of what I do and it is in everyone's nature to take on other people's barnacles really. The question is what do you want or what do you need when you feel those barnacles weighing you down. Where has your boat taken you? How can you create as many perfectly formed crystals for yourself and others while you have the energy and the creative power to do so? *The tongue has the power of life and death and those who love it will eat its fruit.* Proverbs 18:21

www.ingramcontent.com/pod-product-compliance
Lightning Source LLC
Chambersburg PA
CBHW071104090426
42737CB00013B/2478